ta-
ive
)le,
r, a

—C. K. ROBERTSON

Canon to the Presiding Bishop of The Episcopal Church;
Editor of *Religion as Entertainment*

"I've always considered science fiction to be the quintessential literature of our species, because it is the only literature to fully address what most makes us human: our ability to engage the cosmos. Religion is another way of doing this, and James McGrath explores these intersections in a provocative and erudite book that not only calls on a variety of human religions, but science fiction on both page and screen."

—PAUL LEVINSON

Author of *The Plot to Save Socrates*

"Those of us who enjoy science fiction take its nature very seriously. And those of us who are excited by Christian faith take the Bible very seriously. There is therefore no better commentator to explore the relationship between theology and science fiction than James McGrath, a serious biblical scholar and science fiction fan who embodies the joy and excitement of the relationship in this accessible and insightful book."

—DAVID WILKINSON

Principal of St. John's College, Durham University

"Refuting the dichotomies that have plagued so much writing on religion, theology, and science fiction, and refusing simply to press one in service of the other, James McGrath weaves a wonderfully nuanced tale of two of humankind's most important and influential ways of imagining our place in the universe—and the place of the universe in our imagination. Few interested in this relationship can afford to miss this book."

—DOUGLAS E. COWAN

Author of *Sacred Space: The Quest for Transcendence in Science Fiction Film and Television*

THEOLOGY AND SCIENCE FICTION

CASCADE COMPANIONS

The Christian theological tradition provides an embarrassment of riches: from Scripture to modern scholarship, we are blessed with a vast and complex theological inheritance. And yet this feast of traditional riches is too frequently inaccessible to the general reader.

The Cascade Companions series addresses the challenge by publishing books that combine academic rigor with broad appeal and readability. They aim to introduce nonspecialist readers to that vital storehouse of authors, documents, themes, histories, arguments, and movements that comprise this heritage with brief yet compelling volumes.

TITLES IN THIS SERIES:

Reading Augustine by Jason Byassee
Conflict, Community, and Honor by John H. Elliott
An Introduction to the Desert Fathers by Jason Byassee
Reading Paul by Michael J. Gorman
Theology and Culture by D. Stephen Long
Creation and Evolution by Tatha Wiley
Theological Interpretation of Scripture by Stephen Fowl
Reading Bonhoeffer by Geffrey B. Kelly
Justpeace Ethics by Jarem Sawatsky
Feminism and Christianity by Caryn D. Griswold
Angels, Worms, and Bogeys by Michelle A. Clifton-Soderstrom
Christianity and Politics by C. C. Pecknold
A Way to Scholasticism by Peter S. Dillard
Theological Theodicy by Daniel Castelo
The Letter to the Hebrews in Social-Scientific Perspective
    by David A. deSilva
Basil of Caesarea by Andrew Radde-Galwitz
A Guide to St. Symeon the New Theologian by Hannah Hunt
Reading John by Christopher W. Skinner
Forgiveness by Anthony Bash
Jacob Arminius by Rustin Brian
Reading Jeremiah by Jack Lundbom
John Calvin by Donald McKim

THEOLOGY AND SCIENCE FICTION

JAMES F. MCGRATH

 CASCADE *Books* • Eugene, Oregon

THEOLOGY AND SCIENCE FICTION

Cascade Books
An Imprint of Wipf and Stock Publishers
199 W. 8th Ave., Suite 3
Eugene, OR 97401

www.wipfandstock.com

PAPERBACK ISBN: 978-1-4982-0451-4
HARDCOVER ISBN: 978-1-4982-0453-8
EBOOK ISBN: 978-1-4982-0452-1

Cataloguing-in-Publication data:

Names: McGrath, James F.
Title: Theology and Science Fiction | James F. McGrath.
Description: Eugene, OR: Cascade Books, 2016 | Series: Cascade Companions | Includes bibliographical references.
Identifiers: ISBN 978-1-4982-0451-4 (paperback) | ISBN 978-1-4982-0453-8(hardcover) | ISBN 978-1-4982-0452-1 (ebook)
Subjects: LCSH: Science fiction—Religious aspects—Christianity | Theology in literature.
Classification: PN3433.6 M3 2016 (print) | PN3433.6 (ebook)

Manufactured in the U.S.A.   SEPTEMBER 21, 2016

CONTENTS

Preface • vii

1   Introduction • 1

2   Space Can(n)ons and Scriptural Canons • 11

3   Science Fiction against Theology and as
    Theology • 25

4   Theology against Science Fiction and as Science
    Fiction • 51

5   Theology and Science Fiction at the Intersection
    with Philosophy and Ethics • 67

6   Science Fiction and Theology in Dialogue and
    Synthesis • 80

7   Three Theological Science Fiction Short
    Stories • 93

Bibliography • 109

PREFACE

Given the amount of time I now devote to exploring the intersection of science fiction and religion, some may be surprised to learn that it is, in fact, a subject that I have come to in a round-about sort of way, and relatively recently as far as my academic involvement in the subject is concerned. My doctoral work and early teaching experience were both focused in New Testament, with the furthest afield that I branched being the Jewish context of early Christianity. At Butler University, however, I found myself in an environment that required me to stretch myself beyond my usual areas of expertise in order to contribute to the core curriculum in a variety of ways. It also gave me the freedom, as a professor of religion, to stretch beyond the Bible and teach on other topics of interest. As a result, in 2003 I developed a core course on religion and science fiction. I found this subject worked reasonably well in its initial form as a freshman humanities colloquium, but it seemed better suited to become an upper-level elective, and so it is in that form that I have since continued to offer the course every few years. I always like to find ways to do research on the subjects about which I teach, and so I accepted an invitation to contribute to a volume on *Religion as Entertainment*, seized the opportunity to present a conference paper on *The Matrix*, and before I knew it, I was trying to assemble an edited volume of my own, *Religion and Science Fiction*, which brought together a wide array of disciplinary perspectives around the subject.

Since that time, the exploration of the intersection of science fiction in all its varied forms, and religion in all its varied forms, has taken off and continued to grow exponentially. This book marks my first book-length treatment of the topic on my own rather than as part of a multi-editor volume. But I am grateful to all those who have contributed to previous volumes that I put together, and in doing so have inspired me to continue thinking and writing in this area. I remain grateful to Butler University for the privilege of teaching and researching in this area. I am also grateful to my Butler colleagues—Brent Hege, Royce Flood, and Franny Gaede—for both discussions of this topic in general over the years, and feedback on this manuscript more specifically. There are also academics from other institutions with whom I've interacted over the years, too many to name them all. And from beyond the academy I am grateful to friends and family who provided opportunities to discuss ideas, and in so doing ensure that I approach this topic in a way that remains accessible to a general audience. From among these I am especially grateful to Rose La Vista and Dawn Shea. I would also like to offer special thanks to my wife Elena for tolerating my love of science fiction (which, alas, she does not share), and to my son Alex for sharing my interest, and in so doing rekindling my own enjoyment of the genre over and over again.

1

INTRODUCTION

A LIGHT SHINES DOWN from heaven. Beings from above descend to Earth, take hold of a human male, and return to the place from whence they came, ascending with him. Where they take him, he sees wondrous and horrific things. He learns that in the celestial realm, as in the earthly, there are beings who stand for good and beings who stand for evil. He has confirmed to him what he had already believed—that those beings, good and evil, are not only at war with one another somewhere above the skies, but are involved in terrestrial affairs. Some of that involvement has set human history on course for a terrible end. Once he is returned to earth, the celestial traveler tries to share his knowledge with others, but many scoff at his message. But he writes a book about his experience, in the hope that some will listen.

Is this a summary of a modern story about an alien abduction, or of an ancient apocalyptic work? The fact that it could be either highlights the parallels between much ancient and contemporary storytelling, and the unbroken tradition that connects them. I have introduced the subject of "theology and science fiction" in this way, as the ground-work for plotting a course ahead through the subject of this book, because it would be easy to miss the extent to which theology and science fiction have at times told much the same story. Doing justice to the intersection of theology and science fiction must entail taking the distinctive characteristics of each seriously, as well as recognizing those instances in which there scarcely seems to be any distinction at all.

One popular approach to theology and sci-fi is content to do what we have done above, namely to note parallels between recent books or movies on the one hand, and Biblical or other sacred literature on the other. Indeed, in some circles it is popular to look for "Christ figures" and religious symbols in popular culture, so as to turn stories into allegories or illustrations of religious teachings. This book will not be approaching the relationship of theology and science fiction in that way, for several reasons. First of all, merely noticing similarities is the most superficial level of treatment of the topic, and those who are content with it can find it in plenty of other places. It is also very easy to read parallels into stories in ways that do not detect symbolism in them, so much as impose a particular religious standpoint as the framework for reading, in a way that risks distorting both in the process.

In this book we will try to look deeper at the way that stories themselves tackle theological ideas, sometimes giving expression to the theological vision of the author, in others simply articulating the religious outlook of characters in the stories in the interest of making them seem more realistic. We will also look at the intersection of science fiction with the formulation of theology in the present, as traditional religions discuss topics such as life on other worlds, or whether machines deserve rights or could even have a "soul." Theology can be expressed in and through science fiction, and science fiction can provide opportunities for the exploration of theological ideas. But before we begin to explore the relationship, we need to first say at least a little about precisely what is meant by the words used in the title of this book.

WHAT IS THEOLOGY?

Whole books have been written about the task of theology, and so readers without at least some background in this area are encouraged to seek more information elsewhere. But it is necessary to say a little here, by way of introduction, about what theology means in the context of the present book, and what it does not. Theology, in terms of its etymology, sounds like it could mean the "study of God," just as biology studies life and living things. But no one has access to God in a way that would allow God to be placed under a microscope and examined. Indeed, many theologians would emphasize that any being, entity, or reality that can be studied and grasped by the human mind is by definition *not* God (with a capital "G") and unworthy of the label. That stance, however, itself assumes a certain theological axiom, namely that there is one God who is greater than human thoughts can conceive and transcends what human words could ever hope to describe. But that definition is not the only one possible. We therefore need to define "theology" here in a manner that encompasses not just one view of the divine, but many possible ones, even as specific theologies may then proceed to offer definitions and to specify attributes of the divine. For the purpose of the present volume, theology may be defined as systematic thought about one's own beliefs about the divine, spirituality, and/or other religious matters.

The aim here is to discuss ways that diverse theologies may engage with science fiction, not to offer an engagement exclusively from one particular theological perspective. As an academic discipline, theology is often contrasted with religious studies, the latter representing the study of religions mostly by outsiders, while theology is defined as the articulation of a religion's perspective from the point of view of an insider. Yet even though this volume is not written to advocate one community's view of God in relation to science fiction, that does not make it a book that is better described as being about *religion* and science fiction. Theology in the present age can scarcely be done in a serious manner without taking into account the viewpoints of religious others who are our neighbors in both the literal geographic sense as well as in cyberspace. And so one can engage with science fiction as well as with the contemporary terrestrial religious other simultaneously, just as one may encounter fictional religions in sci-fi that may more closely resemble one's own religion or that of others found in the world in the present day. This book seeks to provide a guide to readers that will help them as they reflect on their own beliefs, and consider those of others, in relation to science fiction, which often provides fictional stories about dealing with entities who are religiously other as well as biologically different from humans.

WHAT IS SCIENCE FICTION?

Science fiction is not quite as hard to define as religion, but it isn't straightforward either. Are works of dystopian futurism "science fiction" even if science does not feature prominently in the story? What if a work is set in a dystopian future in which not only is there no new science, but even much present science has been forgotten? Are superhero comic books science fiction? What about James Bond and other spy thrillers which feature gadgets that did not really exist at the time the story was written? If a TV show depicts people traveling using teleportation technology that could probably never exist in reality, some might challenge its right to be called *hard* science fiction. But what makes it science fiction at all?

If there is a key distinction to make in relation to science fiction, it is distinguishing it from the genre of fantasy. Both are sometimes placed under the broader heading of "speculative fiction." But the distinction between fantasy and sci-fi is important as it relates to our interest in religion and theology. One can find many of the same elements in both—worlds different from our own, inhabited by beings like ourselves (often with minor differences like pointed ears), as well as terrifying and dangerous monsters, and the use of weapons that at least seem like magic. The difference is that, in science fiction, the quasi-humans may be called *aliens* rather than *elves*, the monsters will likewise be alien animals, and instead of casting spells that fire lightning, one will use a laser rifle. It is the positing of a scientific explanation for these unreal beings and occurrences that distinguishes sci-fi from fantasy. But the distinction is a blurry one, in the sense that there does not need to be a *plausible* scientific explanation that seems valid based on our current understanding, but merely the assertion that things are realized by scientifically explicable means, rather than actual magic.

And so, minimally, it would seem that any stories in which science—or things which purport to be scientific—feature prominently deserve to be placed in the category of science fiction. Just as one can debate endlessly about what precisely is or is not *religion*, so too can one debate what deserves to be called science fiction. Fortunately, we can set aside such debates, as there are plenty of uncontroversial examples that could fill a much larger book than this one. But the rejection of magic on the part of most sci-fi, while embracing it under a quasi-scientific guise, is important to keep in mind as a common feature in science fiction. We will find that many sci-fi stories overlap with and even borrow from earlier traditions of storytelling which featured the mythical and the magical. Religion has also regularly sought to distinguish itself from magic, albeit in very different ways and along different lines. And as we proceed, we will find that both religion and science fiction have a more ambiguous relationship to magic and myth than either tends to acknowledge.

Before proceeding, it is worth mentioning that this book will avoid focusing in detail on specific stories. Instead it aims to explore questions and themes that pervade a great deal of science fiction literature, television, and film, using specific stories as examples and illustrations. That way, it shouldn't matter whether you have read or seen this or that story or television show, making the book more useful to a wider array of readers. Focusing on the details of specific stories would risk unnecessarily alienating the reader (pun intended).

WHAT IS THEOLOGY AND SCIENCE FICTION?

There are a great many different ways to relate theology and science fiction. One can approach sci-fi through the lens of one's own theological assumptions, and treat the text (whether written or cinematographic) as a place to find culturally relevant illustrations of one's own beliefs. Or, alternatively, if the stories are not malleable enough to allow one to find support for one's own ideas in them, one can criticize the stories because they oppose one's own belief system. One can also ask questions about authorial intention, often more easily addressed in relation to sci-fi than ancient sacred texts, because in many cases the authors of the former are still living, while in other cases, merely by virtue of having lived more recently in history, we have more evidence about their views than we have for specific ancient authors, or even entire human cultures of the past. One can also eschew questions about what authors intended and focus on the imaginary world within the text itself, adopting a narrative approach and asking about gods, rituals, and beliefs within the world of the text. And one can look at ways that science fiction stories inspire people to believe and to act in the real world in ways that are at least quasi-religious, and which incorporate theological elements.

One may also ask about the appropriate response to science fiction, and how it compares to the responses to important stories in religious settings. Are science fiction stories—and any theology expressed in them—supposed to be "believed"? Is the suspension of disbelief involved in reading stories in this genre different from what is involved in reading the Bible or the Ramayana or another sacred text, and if so, in what way? Science fiction provides wonderful opportunities to discuss the nature of narrative and of belief in relation to religion. Kronos was the Greek god of time, and not just a character on *Doctor Who*. When ancient people first depicted time as devouring his children, was this thought of as a literal story about what happened once in ages past, or as a picture of the way time constantly produces things and yet also eventually destroys them? Can we know the answer to this question, given that we have stories which well antedate the time in which these characters were first spoken of? And, given that there were subsequent interpretations of such stories in both a literal and an allegorical fashion in the Greek tradition, what does it indicate that *Doctor Who* chose to incorporate this entity as a character that literally exists in the fictional world the show depicts?[1]

MODELS OF INTERACTION BETWEEN THEOLOGY AND SCIENCE FICTION

Ian Barbour is well known for having delineated a number of different possible approaches to the relationship between theology or religion on the one hand, and science on the other.[2] These can usefully be adapted to the relationship between theology and science fiction. The two may be seen as in conflict, as having nothing to do with one another, as having potential for dialogue between them, or as ideally to be integrated into a unified whole. There have been examples of science fiction authors and of theologians who would embrace each of these models. We advocate here, however, just as Barbour does, for certain kinds of interaction being preferable to others. Since science fiction is literature which imagines humanity's future and the role science will play in it, the only way to declare them as inherently in conflict is to say that humanity will have to choose between religion and science, and that only one can be part of its future. That is, of course, precisely what some have depicted in their stories, but the mere ability to portray something does not immediately render it either likely or preferable to alternatives. In much the same way, to treat theology and science fiction as having nothing to say to one another is to suggest that either science or religion has nothing useful

1. See Leonhardt, *Jewish Worship in Philo*, 68–69, 289–90, on the way Philo of Alexandria makes use of Roman traditions about Kronos/Saturn. Kronos appears in the *Doctor Who* episode "The Time Monster" (S9/E5).

2. See for instance his *When Science Meets Religion*, 1–4.

to contribute to humanity's future. If one regards religion and science as non-overlapping magisteria (to use Stephen Jay Gould's phrase)—as completely distinct spheres of human life each with its own separate validity—it nonetheless remains the case that *fiction* which finds one or the other utterly superfluous to its story is suggesting that a major aspect of historic human expression has no place in the future being imagined.[3] And so, at the very least, the two ought to be in conversation, and indeed, science fiction ought to be one of the places in which and around which the conversations between theology and science actually take place. However, the case can be made that, in fact, the best scenario is one of integration, one in which we find ourselves able to incorporate insights from both science fiction and religion in our theological reflection, and to incorporate science and theology in our storytelling and our thinking about the future and about humanity's role in the cosmos. For evidence that this is the best scenario, one needs to do little more than look at some of the most interesting and engaging science fiction, from the very beginnings to the present day, and one will find that theological themes are woven into their very core—provided one understands theology not as a narrow sectarian enterprise, but as asking questions and exploring mysteries related to the nature of existence, of transcendence, and of meaning.[4]

This book aims to help readers explore the theological ideas in science fiction stories, and the intersection of those stories with modern theological concerns and issues as well. It should therefore be just as useful for those who adopt a religious studies approach as a theological one, since religious studies still examines the ideas, beliefs, concepts, and symbols that religious traditions use. But the book will also

3. Gould, "Nonoverlapping Magisteria," 16–22.
4. On this point see further Cowan, *Sacred Space*.

be useful for those who want to engage science fiction in relation to a theological tradition of their own. Each chapter will end with questions intended to assist the reader in reflecting further. But anyone who knows theology and/or science fiction will know that questions will arise every step along the way.

QUESTIONS FOR REFLECTION

- Is your interest predominantly in either theology or science fiction rather than equally in both? How do you think your interests and background might influence your view of how to relate the two?

- What are some of your favorite science fiction stories, shows, and films? Which are you aware of but have never read or seen? What theological tradition has shaped you personally and your immediate cultural context? What other theological traditions are you aware of but have never studied them? How might your own specific experience and perspective influence your exploration of this topic?

2

SPACE CAN(N)ONS
AND SCRIPTURAL CANONS

THE TERM "CANON" IS used to denote the list of texts which
are considered to be part of sacred scripture for Jews and
Christians, and sometimes other religious traditions as
well. It is also used to denote those books, episodes, and/or
movies which are considered to represent the official story
in a particular science fiction franchise. A canon in the former sense is discussed and appealed to in most theological
discussions in those traditions that regard a particular corpus of literature as having special importance. Therefore,
even before seeking to relate the theological and science
fictional enterprises to one another, we can already begin
to glean insights from the terminological intersection of
the two around the concept of "canon." For convenience,
we will draw most of our examples from two franchises
about which there has been much discussion of their canons in recent years: Star Wars and Doctor Who. However, it

should be clear from these examples how these points apply more broadly.

In the case of the Bible, the term "canon" has to be used in the plural, and even then it is not unproblematic. There are different Jewish, Catholic, Orthodox, Protestant, Ethiopic, and other Bibles, with lists of contents that differ at least somewhat. And even when a list is agreed upon, issues of text and translation come into play. If a reading is in a footnote of a translation, is it canonical? What if it appears in many Greek texts but is not even acknowledged in a footnote in your New Testament? Scribal alterations both accidental and intentional complicate the question of canon, and the release of special edition versions of the *Star Wars Trilogy, Episodes IV, V,* and *VI* has had a similar impact. One can agree on what works constitute canon in the *Star Wars* universe, and yet not agree about whether Han shot first. And of course, even within a canon with clearly defined texts, the presence of different authors and screenwriters also contributes to diversity and contradictions. George Lucas's attempt to make Han Solo a more ethical hero by not having him kill Greedo in cold blood (or, if you prefer, in a "preemptive strike") is comparable to what the Chronicler did with David, when he simply left out details such as David's rape of Bathsheba and arrangement for the murder of her husband. Rewriting and revision can happen not only *to* canonical works, but also *among* canonical works. Copyists may introduce changes into a work, but so too may authors who use the earlier work as a source, in some cases producing new compositions that end up sitting side by side with their source material within the same canon.

Canons inevitably contain material with some degree of diversity among them. For this reason, it is axiomatic that religious communities will consider some canonical works more authoritative or more relevant than others, and read them more frequently, so that they have a greater influence as a result. This is always true in practice, even if it is not always acknowledged. One popular way of referring to this phenomenon is to speak of Christian communities having a "canon within the canon." Pentecostals may focus more attention on Acts and 1 Corinthians; Lutherans may read Romans and Galatians more frequently; Roman Catholics may insist that there is nothing strawy about the Letter of James. Likewise, devout *Star Wars* fans may differ on the extent to which they treat the prequels as on the same par as the original trilogy; one may be a sort of *Doctor Who* Marcionite nowadays, calling oneself a fan without ever having seen an episode of the show prior to those starring Christopher Eccleston.

Whose authority determines what is and isn't canonical, and how those works which are deemed canonical are to be "correctly" interpreted? This varies in the realms of both religion and science fiction. In some denominations, the church is recognized as the authority that determined the canon, purportedly under divine guidance. In other denominations, it is claimed (rather implausibly, for those who know the history) that the canon was as divinely ordained as the words of the texts themselves and that the church, ultimately, had nothing to do with it. The question of how a canon of scripture relates to the deity about which those scriptures speak is one that is not always addressed directly and explicitly in religious communities. Could it be that here at last we have found an aspect of religious canons that is unparalleled in science fiction? Not really. Although the one mind behind the *Star Wars* franchise is a human one rather than a divine one (in the view of almost all fans, at any rate), the relationship between this one mind and that of the actual scriptwriters (such as Leigh Brackett and

Lawrence Kasdan in the case of *The Empire Strikes Back*, for instance) is not always clear. And even if literal divinity is not ascribed to creators and producers of science fiction, it is nonetheless the case that the term for an authorial pronouncement about meaning (often appealed to in order to settle debates among fans about the interpretation of a story) is "the Word of God."[1]

In the case of religious texts, it often happens that "the Word of God" comes to be identified with the texts themselves. But in most cases—and the biblical tradition is a good example of this—a distinction between the two was made at least initially. The biblical literature emerged out of traditions that included roles for prophetic figures who claimed to deliver the "Word of God" verbally, in a live performance rather than in writing. And because of the confusion that can be created when prophetic figures enter into conflict and contradict one another, it often happens that prophetic religions develop with time into religions of the book. Few today have experience of what it must have been like to inhabit a religious tradition in which a new prophetic utterance had the potential to unseat, upend, or at the very least change one's perspective on earlier oracles. But those who watch sci-fi television may have a sense of what it might be like to await weekly oracles that expand a tradition's corpus of authoritative utterances. And fans of long-running film franchises with significant gaps between movies know the sense of anticipation—of hope and fear—that comes with the announcement that a new movie will be made. But what happens when there is tension within the tradition among authority figures, such as when none other than George Lucas himself voices qualms about a new *Star Wars* film, made after he passed the baton of the

1. See the article "Word of God" on the TV Tropes website: http://tvtropes.org/pmwiki/pmwiki.php/Main/WordOfGod.

franchise to Disney? Whose authority is considered paramount—that of the original creator, or that of the current owner? Or is it ultimately the fans who decide?

The notion of a closed canon—or even of an open canon to which only certain authorized individuals can contribute—is problematic in a number of ways. Even when there are clear hierarchical structures in place (whether they be schools of prophets in the king's employ or executive producers), in practice, someone with charismatic rather than institutional authority may have their words become part of the canon by popular acclamation, even if never officially included in the list of canonical stories. There are other ways that the distinction between official and unofficial can be transgressed. Someone who was once merely a fan can come to play the Doctor. Another fan can offer some speculation in an online chat forum, and later write it into an episode if that person becomes the show's producer.[2] Moreover, canons by definition have permeable edges, because literature simply cannot exist in complete isolation from existing languages and cultural tropes, to say nothing of actual literary works. What happens when a work that becomes canonical makes reference to or quotes a work that is not included in the canon? *Doctor Who* fans have debated this since the minisode "The Night of the Doctor" featured the Eighth Doctor making reference to companions who have never appeared or been mentioned before in televised episodes, but are to be found in *Doctor Who* audiobooks. Does this mention of them render those audiobooks canonical? Not necessarily. We see something

---

2. Both scenarios have become realities on *Doctor Who*. Peter Capaldi is not the first person to take on the role after having previously been a fan of the show himself. And Steven Moffatt may or may not be the first to have turned one of his own fan theories into a story element.

very similar in the case of Jude's "minisode" in the New Testament, which quotes from 1 Enoch, a text which nonetheless remains extracanonical for most Christians. Similarly, I have yet to find anyone who thinks that Cleanthes's "Hymn to Zeus" or Aratus's *Phaenomena* ought to be considered canonical simply because they are quoted in Acts 17. Such examples illustrate that canonical boundaries are blurry and permeable.

Even though the authors of the New Testament may be presumed not to have anticipated that their own works would one day achieve canonical status, they wrote in a manner that sought to achieve at least an impression of continuity and coherence with those works which already had canonical status in their time, the Jewish Scriptures.[3] In science fiction and other related genres, "retroactive continuity" ("retcon" for short) refers to the practice of making later developments that appear to be at odds with earlier statements fit by reinterpreting the earlier statements. Examples abound in science fiction. But we can also consider the concept of fulfilment of prophecy in Christianity (to the extent that this is understood to involve prediction rather than typology) as an example of retconning. Isaiah 53 is just like every other text in the Hebrew Bible inasmuch as it had nothing to do with Jesus when it was written. However, Christian retconning has been so effective that Isaiah 53 is considered by many today to be an amazing prediction about Jesus, with few Christian readers recognizing that in its original context it had a different meaning. The text does not offer specific details that uniquely match the historical experience of Jesus when he died, but rather matches the

3. The precise boundaries, especially of the writings, may have still been fluid, but the Torah and the prophets were widely agreed upon in terms of their scriptural contents by this time.

theological interpretation of his death that was offered by Christians after the fact.

The issue of coherence does not go away after the stage of textual composition is completed. Subsequent interpreters may also desire to eliminate the appearance of contradictions within a canonical body, and will find ways to achieve harmonization, often going to great lengths and proposing extremely arbitrary or forced interpretations in order to do so. With its fifty years of history, *Doctor Who* has had plenty of time and opportunity to produce contradictions; the same is true of the decades that saw the production of the New Testament works, and the centuries over which the works of the Hebrew Bible were composed. In all these cases, the contradictions can be so blatant as to make one wonder whether the authors in question were even attempting to remain part of the same franchise at all. Be that as it may, left with contradictions within narratives, fans of *Doctor Who* and of the Bible have found incredibly convoluted ways to attempt to achieve harmonization. What can we learn by comparing the two—whether the creative solutions offered by inerrantist Whovians and Christians, or the ability to live with unresolved contradiction on the more liberal ends of both traditions? And what does it say about fans and followers if contradictions between stories—whether between the infancy stories in Matthew and Luke, or the situation of Gallifrey in the End of Time and the Day of the Doctor—may not even be noticed by some, while they may seem obvious and important to others?

The phenomenon of "headcanon" deserves to be mentioned at this juncture, as it relates to television and film much as the oral Torah relates to the written. "Headcanon" denotes those things which an individual fan, or fans in general, deduce or assume to be true even though not explicitly stated in the canonical works. Did Luke Skywalker stop fighting his father when he did in *Return of the Jedi* because he thought that he had reached a point of balance and wanted to avoid the dark side even if it meant failure? Or did he do so because he believed that the key to victory was to force (pun intended) his father to save him, coming back from the dark side and discovering the goodness still within him in the process? Or could it have been both? Or was there some other reason? *Return of the Jedi* does not tell us, at least not explicitly. The assumptions viewers make and the implications they deduce will have the status of "headcanon." No one watches TV or film without deducing, assuming, and imposing. This is an accepted tenet of modern scholarship about literature and other media. As readers we do not simply obtain meanings encoded in texts by authors. We *make* meaning, we impose and assume and deduce and in other ways interpret. And yet there are readers of literature in general, and the Bible in particular, who deny that they are doing anything other than reading and understanding what is there. Perhaps reference to the issues that appear—and in this case are usually explicitly recognized as matters of interpretation—in the context of sci-fi fandom can help make clear that this is also happening in the case of the Bible.

It is fandom—communities of faithful followers of films and shows or of the Bible—that leads to ongoing interpretation, which in turn regularly leads to the production either of further texts that become canonical, or texts which remain extracanonical but are nonetheless enjoyed by the faithful, and which thus both reflect and in turn shape their interpretation of the canonical text. We see this in the retellings of the Exodus story in Jewish tradition, some details of which are echoed in the Mosaic imagery utilized by Matthew in his infancy narrative. Is there a fundamental difference between a novel about the earlier life of the Doctor on Gallifrey, and extracanonical stories about Jesus as a child in Galilee, or as a young adult in India? Headcanon written down and elaborated on in narrative form becomes fanfic—better known in other contexts as Midrash or rewritten Bible.

Canon is complicated not only *within* a tradition but also *across* traditions. There have been crossover comics bringing together the realms of *Star Trek* and *Doctor Who*, for instance. That raises the question of the extent that comics represent canon. Yet if there is a sense in which some or all of them may be extracanonical from the perspective of the film or TV franchise producers, the comics may still be considered canonical within a branch of fandom that favors comics, just as the influence of extracanonical gospels on Christian art shows the weight those stories had in some communities. But here we are still dealing with branches of the same tradition, much as readers of the Gospel of Peter or the Gospel of Truth belonged to branches of the same tradition as those who read only one or more of the gospels that became canonical. But texts and stories can cross over to other traditions entirely, such as when a story known from the Infancy Gospel of Thomas also appears in the Qur'an.[4] Does the appearance of the Doctor on the Enterprise make the entire Whovian corpus canonical to Trekkies, or vice versa? Not necessarily. When Mani, or the Qur'an, affirms books and/or key figures from biblical tradition, it is emphatically *not* an embrace of the entirety of the Jewish and/or Christian canons without qualification. One may bring another canon (or elements thereof) within one's own either to affirm it, or to subordinate it. And indeed, one might refer to Christianity's relationship to Judaism, or Manichaeism's relationship to Christianity, in terms of a

4. Surah 3:49; 5:110.

"reboot"—starting a new franchise that takes up an existing story and characters but envisages them in a new way.

Picking and choosing is a phenomenon that happens across all aspects of fandom and faithful religiosity, both within and outside of a canon. It happens when the makers of *Doctor Who* decide to make him half human on his mother's side, and then decide to eliminate that from the canon, only to have it mentioned on the show yet again as a real possibility. It happens when a papal pronouncement appears to those outside the Catholic Church to contradict an earlier papal pronouncement. It happens when *Star Wars* fans decide that Jar Jar and/or Ewoks spoil the fictional universe they love, and take pleasure in denigrating them, or merely ignore their existence. And it happens when American Catholics use birth control. Selectivity is an inherent part of healthy human existence. If we could detect every wavelength of light and sound, and have every memory fresh in our recall, we could not function. The fundamentalist may deny both the legitimacy of picking and choosing, and that they actually do it, but it is the responsibility of those who study theology to know better, and to try to help people avoid self-delusion in their fandom and/or their religiosity.

What leads someone to spend hours upon hours trying to harmonize *Star Wars Episodes I* and *IV*, or the Book of Revelation with the Book of Daniel, and what does a comparison between the two help us to see that looking at one or the other on its own might not? In both cases, individuals and communities are using texts to make meaning in their own lives, to interpret the world they inhabit, to find hope for the future, and to convey values that are important to their worldview.

The practice of religion in fact has many points of comparison with the rituals of the most devout fans, who will make pilgrimages to meet their icons, dressed in sacred garb that allows them to imagine they are part of the sacred stories. Of course, pilgrimage and special raiment are not part of all religious traditions. So too, there are many different ways of approaching theology, and many different ways of being a science fiction fan. There are many different things that readers hope to get out of watching television episodes or of reading the Bible. Our approach in this volume, which embraces the results of academic scholarship in approaching theology, is but one option. It is a value judgment (one that we do not have space and time to defend here) that one will better appreciate the Bible, or science fiction, if one recognizes the human activities that weave and create the universes in question, with all their shortcomings and contradictions. We have all seen the harm that fundamentalism can cause. The unwillingness to see good in the worldviews of others, and the unwillingness to see the shortcomings in one's own, can lead to any number of emotional responses to the other that can in turn cause great harm. This is true whether the tribe one is attacking or defending is one of religion or of fandom—although one of these more frequently leads to violence than the other, and it is worth asking why that should be the case, as it may help us to better identify the distinctions between the two, and at precisely what point the parallels break down.

A scholarly approach to sacred texts or sci-fi must be open to recognizing problems and contradictions, but that does not mean it aims to tear down literature that others appreciate. The low budget special effects in *Doctor Who* in the 1960s are simply an aspect of what its human producers had to make do with, and can even be a reason to appreciate what they did with those limited resources, rather than a reason for mockery. And yet sometimes, confronted with the ideology of the devout fan, one may be tempted to make snide remarks about the use of spray-painted bubble wrap as a prop, or the fact that a camera operator is visible in a scene. And sometimes, confronted with the ideology of a devout religious fundamentalist, one may be tempted to make snide remarks about the assumption that the Earth has a dome above it with lights embedded in it. Sometimes poking fun can be the only way to burst the bubble of a viewpoint that has rendered itself otherwise impervious to criticism. If we go too far, though, we cease to be engaged in the effort to combat fundamentalist thinking, but may be veering in the direction of an equal if opposite fundamentalism ourselves. One of the benefits of comparing science fictional and biblical canons is that it may help us to see and reflect on how we approach not just these subject matters, but the values at work in our theological undertaking.

The level of commitment to a franchise or collection of texts does not necessarily correlate with the level of honesty about the issues talked about in this chapter. Fans are sometimes delineated using terms like "*casual* fans, *fairweather* fans, and *diehard* fans."[5] We can likewise talk about casual, fair-weather, and diehard religionists. It is possible to be ignorant of academic perspectives on the Bible and/or science fiction and be in any of these categories; it is possible to take scholarship on any of them seriously and be in any of the categories. This volume does not aim to be prescriptive with respect to theology, but to provide a guide to interacting between and among one's own theological and science fictional interests. Different readers will have different authorities. But it is worth highlighting that ultimately all authorities—whether they be J. J. Abrams, the Bible, George Lucas, Pope Francis, or Steven Moffatt—only have authority inasmuch as individuals and communities grant that authority. That is perhaps the most important thing

5. Hirt and Clarkson, "Psychology of Fandom," 61.

that can be illustrated through a comparison of science fiction and biblical canons. Fans may use "the word of God" to refer to authorial statements of intent and meaning. But that doesn't mean that any fans will *always* defer to such authorities, nor does it mean that all fans will do so at least sometimes. The Bible only has authority inasmuch as it is read and accepted. Given that its contents are not uniform, it is crucial that people be aware that the real authority lies not with the Bible, but with the one using it. Somewhat ironically, the authority rests precisely with those who give their authority away to others, accepting uncritically the statements of those who interpret the Bible for them, whether because they mistakenly believe the claim of those individuals to be merely repeating "what the Bible says," or because they consider that the individuals in question have a unique right to act as interpreters. The big problem when it comes to biblical literacy and so-called biblical authority is not the mere rejection of scholarship about the Bible, but the rejection of all we know about how canons come into existence, and the human roles at work in producing the texts, collecting them, and interpreting them. A comparison of the canons of the Bible and science fiction franchises can be useful in helping to make these points clear. Drawing attention to the roles that canons play in science fiction and in theology is a useful stepping stone on the way to the kinds of engagement between the two that we aim for in the subsequent chapters of this book.

QUESTIONS FOR REFLECTION

- What is a canon and how is it defined in relation to scripture and to science fiction? In what ways are the two comparable, and how are they different?

- What makes it desirable to have a canon? What are the disadvantages and problems that arise when an individual or community seeks to distinguish between works that are canonical and others that are non-canonical?

3

SCIENCE FICTION AGAINST THEOLOGY AND AS THEOLOGY

SCIENCE FICTION HAS A reputation for being antagonistic to religion; however, the reputation is not entirely deserved, and even where the description seems to fit, it often represents at best an oversimplification. On *Star Trek*, the Enterprise (like most science fiction starships) lacked a chaplain, and its crew seemed to have no expressed need for religious beliefs or practices. Various sci-fi franchises have depicted humanity encountering its gods in deep space, only to learn that they were aliens—and typically not very nice ones. Science fiction has often been perceived as literature, television, and film specifically for people who choose science rather than superstition, with religion placed under the latter heading. When it has depicted religious characters, they have often been fundamentalists of one sort or another—and that includes the Cylons in the rebooted *Battlestar Galactica*.

But when we scratch beneath the surface, we find that matters are much more complex. Science fiction has, in fact, been replete with nuanced as well as not-so-nuanced religious themes throughout its history. Ray Bradbury depicted missionaries sent from Earth to Mars in several of his stories, and these characters reflected seriously on the nature of religious truth and religious experience. The same may be said of the character of Father John Carmody, a central character in a number of stories by Philip José Farmer. But even works that appear disinterested in religion or even hostile to it at first glance may have something more constructive to say when one looks more closely at the details. After all, attacking religion is not only something that the anti-religious do. It is also something that religions have frequently done and continue to do to one another, understanding the very act of critiquing what are felt to be wrong ideas about the divine to be an expression of religious devotion.

GODS AS ALIENS

While most regard the "ancient aliens" viewpoint as implausible history, it is nonetheless extremely popular as a theme in science fiction storytelling. What can be said about the theology of stories which turn gods into aliens and aliens into gods? Some have viewed them as asserting the falsehood of classic human mythology, demoting powerful spiritual entities to the level of mere biological organisms which, however powerful they might be, can be fought, and whose demands for worship may appropriately be resisted. The topic of what (if anything) makes a being worthy of worship has itself been explored in science fiction, as well as theologians. If particular aliens created humans, or saved us at a particular moment in history, or are supremely powerful or inherently benevolent, would the beings in question merit our worship, or at least our reverence? If they rescued us from disaster, might we not find ourselves quite literally singing their praises? And if merely having been involved in bringing our species into existence does not make a being worthy of worship in science fiction, then presumably one ought not to claim that it does in one's theology about the real world. There have, in fact, been many theologies which have made a point of this sort—for instance Gnosticism, which typically views our material bodies as something negative, and so the being that was responsible for creating them is viewed with hostility, not adoration.

Equally interesting is the fact that, in turning ancient gods into aliens, science fiction stories of this sort make the myths and legends *more literally true* than any historian would judge them. From the perspective of critical scholarship, ancient stories of encounters with gods and angels are viewed with extreme skepticism, or are simply set aside as inherently improbable and thus beyond the purview of historical investigation. Yet in the science fiction stories in question, we are given the impression that, in these myths, ancient humans reported and recorded what they saw with a high degree of accuracy and precision. The real issue separating the modern science fiction tales from the ancient ones is a theological question: whether the beings from above ought to be called "gods." Most modern stories seem to give the answer "no." Yet if (as per Clarke's law) "any sufficiently advanced technology is indistinguishable from magic," then might it not also be said that any sufficiently advanced civilization is indistinguishable from divinity? How might one distinguish the kind of existence that the Q Continuum on *Star Trek* is supposed to have, for instance, from the kind of existence angels and divine beings are depicted in human mythology as experiencing?

Science fiction, far from sounding a death knell to the gods, has populated the heavens with them. And one can go further, asking about different kinds of beings and making comparisons between them. Are beings like Q on *Star Trek* more godlike than the Goa'uld on *Stargate*, and if so, why? Are capriciousness and meddling more or less compatible with divinity than complete self interest and malevolence? Such theological questions are not as easy to answer as might be assumed. Even in monotheistic traditions, there has historically been room for other beings that might or might not be called "gods," but nonetheless fit the historic description, however much it may be emphasized that they are subordinate to one supreme God. Rarely has pure monotheism, in the sense of a single power with no genuine rival, been adopted in an unqualified form. The complexities of life and the ambiguities of existence make stories of genuine conflict between good and evil seem more compelling. And so often the actual distinction between monotheism and polytheism has had to with whether worship is addressed to the beings below the supreme deity at the pinnacle of the celestial hierarchy.[1]

In bringing gods into real existence, albeit in fictional stories, why is science fiction considered to be antagonistic to religion, rather than being viewed as having breathed new life into certain forms of it, by making the existence of the gods more plausible? Perhaps because, in stories ranging from *Star Trek* to *Stargate*, humans consistently refuse to worship the powerful entities that they encounter on their journeys through space, even when those entities demand that they do so. Often, the humans in the story will explicitly insist that the beings they encountered are not gods.

1. On this topic see further McGrath, "Monotheism."

But on what basis do they make this theological assertion? It seems to assume that gods cannot be biological entities that participate in the universe of change. But this assumption has not always been as widely shared by humans as it is today. Ancient Greek gods were thought to have a substance called *ichor* rather than blood coursing through their veins, but that is a far cry from simply being immaterial. In many polytheistic systems, the gods were believed to have emerged from a primordial chaos that produced them, after which those first deities subsequently begat still more gods, who might be *immortal*, but could not be said to be *eternal*. It is not clear why being the result of a process of evolution should make gods less divine, any more than it makes humans less human.

Godhood has sometimes been defined in terms of the attributes of the entity for which divinity is claimed. But others have suggested that it is the actions of others towards a person or thing that turns it into a god. If money, power, and fame can be considered gods or idols, then surely aliens can. Monotheists might insist that these are inappropriate objects of worship because they are less than ultimate, but that too is a theological statement, and one that is not incompatible with the view that the entities worshiped by ancient Egyptians, or Israelites, or Greeks, were real entities that came traveling from space.[2] It is a useful thought experiment for religious people to ask how they would view the events depicted in their scriptures, if those events turned out to be actual historical events brought about by aliens. Would it be appropriate, for instance, to continue to celebrate Passover with gratitude if the entity that freed Hebrew slaves from Egypt long ago was an extraterrestrial

2. And of course, the viewpoint that aliens built the pyramids, or were seen by Ezekiel, has become popular even outside the realm of science fiction. See most famously the writings of Erich von Däniken.

who used a tractor beam to part the sea? Many would instinctively say "no," but explaining precisely *why* we have that gut reaction is more difficult. And even if we were to settle on a negative answer to this question within the framework of our own particular theological system, how certain should we feel that this answer that we have given is the correct one?

MACHINES AS GODS

The expectation that long evolution might have turned other intelligent life in the universe into gods or godlike beings reflects the mythical hope that evolution might one day bestow the same gifts upon us. Such hopes are unrealistic, scientifically speaking. But they reflect a mythologization of evolution in service of what we might call a humanist theology, one that is persuaded of humanity's potential for divinity. It is not only our organic, biological descendants that might one day reach that potential, according to science fiction storytelling. Artificial intelligences also have the potential to evolve into something godlike—and indeed, to get there much more quickly than biological evolution could achieve without interference. Once machines have reached a level of intelligence that surpasses that of their human creators, it can be presumed that they will be able to intervene in their own development, and reproduce themselves in such numbers and at such a pace, that they would then evolve exponentially towards something unimaginable. This is often referred to as the "singularity"—a term also familiar to fans of science fiction because it is also used in physics, in relation to the warping of spacetime towards infinity. This technological possibility for the achievement of divinity unconstrained by the inheritance of biological existence is still fiction at present. But it is something that many futurists consider much more plausible than our evolution of superhero-like abilities through genetic mutations.

Star Trek has shown particular interest in the theme of computers as "false gods," put in place to oversee the lives of biological species in a manner that maintains stability and safety, at the expense of healthy exploration, freedom of thought and action, and other important aspects of human development. In a related way, the *Dune* novels by Frank Herbert depicted humanity's future in a time after a largely successful jihad had been waged against artificial intelligences. Science fiction often adopts a positive view of the potential for humanity to evolve—or to learn to harness currently latent abilities—in order to do things that currently would seem like magic. When it comes to technology that allows us to travel through space and time, to create and destroy, to see and know beyond our current capabilities, there is often greater ambivalence. And when it comes to technologies that are incorporated into ourselves, modifications to humanity which move in the direction of our becoming cyborgs or even leaving our fleshly mode of existence behind altogether, there is typically a high level suspicion at the very least, and often outright rejection of the appropriateness of pursuing such an aim. Yet why should this be the case? Freud referred to humanity as a "prosthetic God" who can achieve many of the things previously ascribed to divinity with the assistance of technology.[3] Why should the ability to explore the distant reaches of the universe—either by unlocking the power of the mind, or by building a starship—be considered appropriate, but not by incorporating the technology to do so into our very persons? Perhaps it is precisely because of the fear that has been part of science fiction since its beginning, of scientists "playing God." In this case, if the abilities really come

3. Freud, *Civilization*, 44.

from within, then perhaps we deserve to be considered divine, and if they are clearly separate from ourselves, the visible technology will serve to remind us that we are not. But when the technology is integrated into us, the lines are blurred, and we are liable to think ourselves more divine than we actually are. Or the concern may be that we will lose that which makes us fundamentally human in the process of integrating technological enhancements into our very persons. The natural course of things is change: if humanity remains as it currently is for millions of years into the future, that would be an anomaly, itself something that could be accomplished only if we remain where we are and actively interfere with the natural process of human evolution. Otherwise, it seems likely that our far distant descendants will be as different from us as we are from organisms that lived the same distance in the past from us.

Or does evolution eventually reach an end point? That suggestion may cause some to bristle, precisely because it sounds like the language of creation and divine providence which religious believers have wished to import into the story of evolution, sometimes to deny the evolutionary narrative altogether, at other times simply to harmonize it with the view of God as Creator. But suggesting that evolution might have an end in the sense of reaching a conclusion need not by definition mean that it has an end in the sense of a goal. Some organisms that have found successful niches for survival have experiences long periods of stasis as a result. If humans can artificially keep our environment the same through the use of technology, is there any reason to expect that our biological form will change radically over time? These are questions that we cannot answer. But they are important ones to think about, scientifically as well as theologically. Therefore, it is to the advantage of humanity that we tell stories that explore and reflect on the potential implications of a wide range of different scenarios.

Maintaining a stable environment will be far more challenging if humanity spreads to other worlds. If we move to worlds that are capable of supporting human life, but are not precisely like Earth, the different gravity or radiation levels or food sources would be as likely to impact our evolution going forward, as radical changes to these aspects of our environment would be to change us over time even if we were on Earth. And, of course, unless we leave Earth, the history of our species cannot be longer than the lifespan of our sun, even assuming that no asteroid strike or other calamity renders the Earth uninhabitable even sooner. Terraforming would be required if we wanted to customize planets so that they suit our current biological form and its needs as well as possible, rather than settling for the alternative of struggling to survive in a less ideal environment in the hope that our descendants in the distant future would one day have evolved to thrive in it. Of course, modifying our genetic makeup deliberately to tailor remake ourselves for new environments is a possibility. But that would involve humanity deliberately becoming multiple species—a fascinating prospect to imagine! If we prefer to change our environment rather than ourselves, that too has implications. Is it appropriate to do so when species already live on a given world? Does it matter whether the species which live there are sentient as humans are? Can we be confident that we can recognize the varied forms that sentience might take on other worlds in other biological organisms? And what happens if other sentient beings much like us have the same plan, and we encounter them as they eagerly seek to transform the same worlds to suit their very different physiology just as we hope to do for ours? If the two aims are at odds, so that making the world hospitable for one sentient species would make it inhospitable for the other, we might find ourselves at war, destroying and damaging worlds instead of bringing new life to them. And indeed, the needs of future descendants of humanity that had previously adapted to different environments could potentially mean that the strange and alien others that we encounter are our own biological relatives. Such scenarios truly are science fictional, set not merely thousands but tens of thousands and even millions of years in the future. But exploring them in the present provides good opportunity to reflect on how we might treat those who truly look and act alien by comparison to another group, and to apply what we learn from that reflection to our interaction with the descendants of humanity with whom we share the planet we now live on, and with whom we ought to be able to find a way to co-exist and thrive together much more easily.

In the Bible, human beings are said to be made "in the image and likeness of God." Theologians typically relate such statements not to humanity's outward appearance (although the author of Genesis may have assumed that humans and divine beings do indeed look similar), but to the cognitive and creative abilities that set us apart from other animals. If we lose our consciousness, our conscientiousness, or our compassion as a result of modifications made to our genes, or technology inserted into our bodies, or even simply by continuing to evolve as a species, this raises serious questions about human nature which have a religious aspect to them. But in the meantime, having technology that can destroy the planet, without the wisdom and maturity to refrain from doing so, presents problems of its own. It is for this reason that science fiction has told story after story about humanity finding itself able to do things, and then actually doing them, before seriously reflecting on whether we *ought* to do them. And that, in turn, is one of the useful functions that science fiction can play in discussions of ethics, as we will explore further in a later chapter. By imagining a future after a nuclear war, or one in which all humans are connected via implants in our brains, we have the opportunity to reflect on whether we ought to aim for or avoid such futures. If it seems obvious that avoiding nuclear war is a good thing, a compelling story about life in the harshness of a nuclear winter may make that truth seem even more self-evident, to a much larger number of people, or simply motivate those who already accept the point to seek to put in place further precautions and safeguards. Imagining a terrible future can be a helpful stepping stone towards avoiding it.

GNOSTICISM

The term "gnostic" has gained currency as a catch-all for a generic kind of spirituality popular in our day and age. But historically, Gnosticism has referred to a more specific religious viewpoint, one that held that the physical world we inhabit is a prison, and the creator thereof a malevolent being who is different from and inferior to the supreme God. In most Gnostic systems of thought, human beings are the prison of a divine spark that originates in the heavenly realm, far above the creator of the material world, and thus of humans' physical bodies. But at death, that spark of light, our true selves, can escape this prison, provided we know the truth and the way, and this is something that can be discovered even while we are still alive in the world.

If some of this description reminds you of *The Matrix* films, you are not alone. In those films, human beings have been enslaved by artificial intelligences which evolved from machines that humans created. To keep us trapped, and useful as a power source, humans are plugged from birth into a virtual reality known as the Matrix. The story focuses on the redeemers who return from the outside world into the Matrix to call people to escape and join them. Of course, these movies also subvert Gnostic ideas, since we learn that the real world outside the Matrix is not a celestial paradise, but a post-apocalyptic nightmare, one to which the deceptive but more pleasant existence in the Matrix can seem like a preferable alternative. The movies thus raise questions about temptation, and whether uncomfortable truths are preferable to a pleasant lie, as well as the ethics of creating artificial intelligences and of how we treat them. The films also provide a good starting point for discussions about the nature of reality, both in relation to virtual reality and the question of whether "real" and "artificial" have any genuine meaning when a whole world can be accurately duplicated in a machine environment, but also in relation to human perception and our ability (or lack thereof) to discern between reality and illusion. That last topic is a major theme in Buddhism and a number of other traditions in addition to Gnosticism.

The *Matrix* movies are by no means the first, nor the only, Gnostic science fiction. Philip Pullman's *His Dark Materials* books also envisage a world under the control of a being who has declared himself supreme, but in fact is not. It might be suggested that any science fiction film that has a universe brought into existence through some experiment or accident has something of the same character, at least to a limited extent. But in some cases the Gnostic elements are deliberate and not just coincidental resemblances. Philip K. Dick famously incorporated Gnosticism in the strict sense into his stories, and indeed into his own worldview as well, to such an extent that he could accurately be described as a Gnostic theologian in the Valentinian tradition.[4]

4. See McKee, *Pink Beams of Light*, 68.

The virtual reality of the *Matrix* has a particularly Gnostic angle to it, with its architect (the Demiurge, i.e., the creator of the material world) and agents (like the archons in Gnostic literature, these block the way of those who seek to escape their prison). Other virtual reality stories, such as *The Thirteenth Floor* and *Vanilla Sky*, lack most of the elements that are specific to Gnosticism. As has already been mentioned, other religious worldviews also regard what we perceive to be reality as an illusion, and call upon people to wake up to the truth. These themes are important in Buddhism and many strands of Hinduism, and deliberate exploration of themes from these traditions—as well as superficial use of their symbols and imagery—can be found in a number of science fiction stories.

THE DIVINE COSMOS

It has already become clear through our survey thus far that monotheistic and polytheistic views (or variations on them) are not the only religious options, whether on Earth in the past and present or in space in the future. And yet some of the alternatives—such as pantheism or panentheism—have been incorporated into sci-fi narratives with far less frequency than the religious traditions which are best known in the English-speaking world. Sometimes a planet or star is found to be sentient, and so might be considered a divinity, much as "Mother Earth" has been so often in human history. But rarely is the view adopted in science fiction that the entirety of the universe might itself be divine, any more than its stories feature the God of classical theism. Characters within the stories may believe such things, but rarely does the story focus on their being accurate. Perhaps this is because it is challenging to tell a plausible and compelling story in which the universe itself is a character. And perhaps this is difficult because most of us do not think about it that way in real life. Yet science fiction regularly explores that which seems fantastic and unreal in terms of our experience in the present, and so there is likely to be some other explanation.

One exception to this general neglect might be the notion of the Force in *Star Wars*. The Force is unlike the monistic concept of Brahman in non-dual forms of South Asian thought, which posit that *all* reality is ultimately one. The Force is not identified in *Star Wars* with all matter, but as an energy that pervades everything, even though not all recognize it or interact with it. A better point of comparison might be the concept of Dao (in the past more often spelled Tao), which gives Daoism (or Taoism) its name. Sometimes rendered into English as "the Way," the Dao is an aspect of reality which pervades all things, but is not necessarily identical to all things, and which is by definition elusive and impossible to pin down. Daoism is famous for the symbolism of Yin and Yang, two opposing forces representing complementary aspects of existence: light and darkness, day and night, male and female, activity and passivity.

It is interesting to ask whether *Star Wars* might be best understood when interpreted through the lens of Daoism. While many understand the light and dark sides of the Force to represent good and evil, in Daoism, neither of the opposing forces is good or evil, but rather what is bad is when these things, each of which has its own rightful place in existence, are out of balance. One can also make reference here to the discussion in Rabbinic Judaism about the good and evil impulse, with at least one rabbi making the argument that the latter is not evil in and of itself—the desires to survive, eat, and procreate are not wrong in themselves, but only when they are followed unchecked.[5] In

5. Genesis Rabbah 9:7.

Star Wars, the Sith emphasize desire and aggression, while the Jedi emphasize detachment and gentleness. Is one right and the other wrong? Or is either unhealthy and unhelpful when taken to its furthest extreme?

There is discussion throughout the Star Wars prequels of a prophecy that one would appear who would bring balance to the Force. The Jedi expected this to involve the destruction of the Sith, but by the end of *Episode III*, we find that Anakin Skywalker (now Darth Vader) has killed all but two Jedi, and so there seem to be only two Jedi and two Sith remaining—a much more balanced situation than that which prevailed previously for a very long time. So too at the end of *Return of the Jedi*, we see Luke Skywalker find that his love and anger can make him stronger, but then he stops attacking at precisely the point at which balance has been achieved—literally a hand for a hand, having cut off his father's hand just as his father had done to him on an earlier occasion. There are debates about whether Star Wars reflects Daoism's idea of opposing forces, which are bad only when either is not balanced by the other, or whether it is closer to Zoroastrianism's idea of two eternal opposing forces which do in fact represent good and evil. This book will not try to settle that matter, since there is probably no definitive answer to be given that could end those debates. The aim here is to encourage the reader to consider more than one interpretation of the films, so that they can participate in such debates, and use the films as a gateway to theological discussion. But hopefully one thing is clear as a result of our discussion: knowledge about religions can help one to make sense of, and explore possible meanings of, elements in science fiction stories.

Another theological viewpoint, known as "radically-emergent theism," also features from time to time in sci-fi. On this view, God is not an eternally-existing entity, nor

THEOLOGY AND SCIENCE FICTION

simply to be identified with the universe, but rather represents a higher order of organization and existence that emerges out of the evolution of the universe. This is perhaps most closely associated with the theology of Pierre Teilhard de Chardin, who spoke of God as the "Omega Point." His theology is explicitly mentioned throughout the four novels of Dan Simmons' *Hyperion Cantos*. But others—both characters within science fiction, and authors and producers thereof—have articulated comparable ideas. For instance, in George Zebrowski's novel *Macrolife*, living things in the universe connect with one another and eventually become part of a higher-order organism. This collective entity that includes what remains of humanity eventually finds a way to survive the destruction of the universe in an impending "big crunch" as gravity leads it to collapse back in upon itself. This entity then joins with entities superior even to them which had survived the similar destructions of previous universes. Together we presume them to share a godlike existence in the next universe to emerge, as the latest collapse leads to another big bang and the process starts all over again, yet with the most advanced entities surviving and crossing over into the newborn universe. It is surely no coincidence that, as the beings hope their plan to survive the end of the universe will work, and that a new universe will emerge, they express that hope in words that echo Gen 1:3: "Let the light begin."[6] The collective godlike entity continues to grow and advance, and yet is understood to be a product of universes rather than their creator. It is an existence that our distant descendants might aspire to participate in themselves. So once again we find science fiction exploring the possibility not only that divinities

---

6. Zebrowski, *Macrolife*, 369.

might really be aliens, but also that humans might one day become divinities.[7]

CREATION

Religion often looms large in the lives of individuals and families at beginnings and endings—at the birth of a child, the marriage of two people to start a new family together, and at death. In parallel with this, religious beliefs often focus particular attention on beginnings and endings, at both the individual and the cosmic level. We will look at ideas like the soul and afterlife in a later chapter, and their intersection with matters of morality and ethics. But cosmic beginnings and endings are every bit as important, if not more so, in many theological systems. We have already explored some concepts of the divine as encountered in science fiction. One important role that defines the divine in some belief systems is that of creator. And so if our universe emerged from an accident in a particle accelerator in some already-existing universe, or if Earth was seeded with life by aliens, do those entities deserve to be called "gods"? Perhaps. But many theologians reserve the term God—at least "God with a capital G"—for that entity that is ultimate, the most transcendent reality which existed before any other. From that perspective, even if one posits alien intelligent designers, the question of where those designers came from remains, as does the question of why there is something rather than nothing in the first place. While such stories, if they turned out to be on the right track, would require some adjustments in existing theologies, they do not eliminate

7. See McGrath, "God Needs Compassion But Not a Starship," in *The Ultimate Star Trek and Philosophy*, on connections between the views discussed here and those of Gene Rodenberry, the creator of *Star Trek*.

the question of what existed before those alien creators, and thus leave some room for God.

The idea of God as simply existing by definition, however, is no more intellectually or logically satisfying than those sci-fi stories featuring a closed causal loop. If our far future descendants discover time travel, and travel back in time to bring our universe into existence, we would be left with no loose ends, and yet would still have a great many questions. How can the past depend for its existence on something or someone from the future, which in turn depends upon that past? Saying "that's just the way things are" fails to satisfy in much the same way that saying "God simply exists by definition" fails to satisfy. Either might turn out to be true, or neither, but bringing the two scenarios into conversation might help us to explore why one kind of explanation satisfies them while another does not. Atheists and religious believers often feel as though their own stance is logical and coherent, while the one they reject is inadequate and unsatisfying. Yet neither manages to eliminate mystery. Perhaps science fiction stories about time travel and causal loops, which leave no loose ends and yet frustrate us immensely, can help both religious people and atheists understand that there is something that is not entirely satisfying, nor apparently definitive, about every possible viewpoint one might have about why anything exists at all, and who or what existed before anything else did.

Stories about scientists bringing universes or life into existence can be composed in an effort to explain how things came to be. As stories about our future, they can also be used to explore ethical questions about what we ought to do, and ought not to do, with our technology. The objection to "scientists playing God" is a frequent one in sci-fi, and it represents another natural point of intersection with theology. Yet this kind of objection has been raised to almost every kind of development in technology, in medicine, and in our scientifically-assisted understanding of the cosmos. If science fiction stories allow us to reflect on possible ethical issues we might face in the future, the history of our storytelling also warns against allowing concerns about "playing God" to interfere with our curiosity and creative exploration of possibilities. Science fiction has presented both utopian and dystopian futures, in which technology has made things better or brought us to the edge of destruction. It is by finding the balance between the two, and appreciating both kinds of stories, that we may hope to find the wisdom to continue pioneering, and yet to refrain from doing so in a way that neglects to reflect adequately on the range of possible implications of our experiments.

THE UNIVERSALITY OF
TRUTH AND ALIEN SALVATION

When civilizations have encountered one another, religious ideas have often been exchanged in the process, whether peacefully or by force. What might happen when terrestrial and extraterrestrial civilizations encounter one another? Not surprisingly, science fiction has a rich diversity of stories exploring such scenarios. Alien religions might prove appealing to humans, whether because they appear to be demonstrably effective in ways that human religions may not be, or because the alien civilization seems more advanced, and so it is assumed that their religious beliefs must be superior, too. This mirrors what has happened at times in human history as empires have spread, and we can see the impact of this in the pages of the Bible, influenced as they are by elements brought to Israel via Babylonia, Persia, and Hellenism, to name a few. What might happen to the ongoing development of Judaism, for instance, if Earth (including its Jewish inhabitants) were to be conquered by aliens with particular religious beliefs? On the one hand, religions often engage in syncretism, borrowing from other traditions, while on the other, even the act of consciously rejecting a particular alternative influences the development of one's own heritage. And so whether human individuals or terrestrial religions respond to encounters with aliens by embracing their ideas or by rejecting them, history suggests that there is no way to avoid being transformed by the encounter.

However, the mere fact that humans and their traditions persist into the future, and spread into space, is no guarantee that we will encounter other intelligent extraterrestrial life forms. What might the far future of current human religions look like, even independently of possible encounters with alien religions? It is a question worth asking. After all, religions change over time, even without much if anything in the way of direct encounter with other systems of thought. Frank Herbert's *Dune* novels famously explored this topic, making reference to specific beliefs, practices, and scriptures that are around at the time the stories are set, tens of thousands of years in humanity's future. What is depicted in those stories is at times realistic, at times blatantly satirical, and at times a bit of both. Such stories provide us with a worthwhile thought experiment. Most people have seen timelines of their own religious tradition, and as much change as has been seen in the past will undoubtedly be seen in the future. But, as with biological evolution, so too with the evolution of theology, its pace is at times so slow that we find it hard to recognize that it is happening all around us, right before our eyes and under our noses. It is only when we look at two snapshots from different times that we are likely to notice just how much has changed. Often science fiction has been insufficiently imaginative, envisioning the same customs being followed a few thousand years from now when people celebrate Christmas on another planet, with songs and customs much as they are today. Even if nothing were to change except the planetary setting, surely the meaning of a story of the birth of a savior changes its connotations when one has to preface it with words like "a long time ago, in a galaxy far, far away."

Christianity is often felt to have the most at stake when it comes to the question of intelligent life elsewhere in the universe. The idea of Jesus as God incarnate raises questions for some Christian theologies, such as whether other planets would also have incarnations, or alternatively, whether the human person Jesus died for beings on other worlds, and if so, whether they await the broadcast of this good news from Earth regarding what God has done to accomplish their salvation. These issues are sometimes raised as though they were an *attack* on Christian theology, as though merely telling a story about this is enough to show how ridiculous the Christian notion of incarnation is. But in fact Christians have been thinking about this topic, and about related or comparable issues, for some time. Indeed, one reason why the discovery of the Americas by Europeans was traumatic was the question it raised, of how God could have allowed there to be humans in parts of the world to which no one was sent with the gospel. The Church of Jesus Christ of Latter-Day Saints addressed this issue by positing both a connection between native Americans and the tribes of Israel, and a visit of the risen Jesus to the Americas. The Mormon tradition has also incorporated many elements that are also found in science fiction into its theology, such as life on other worlds, and unsurprisingly this has also led to there being more than a few Mormons involved in the writing or producing of science fiction.

Ray Bradbury and C. S. Lewis are among those authors who wrote stories about Christians traveling to other worlds in our solar system, encountering sentient life there, and discovering that those worlds did not need to be evangelized. In the case of Bradbury's "The Fire Balloons," it is because those beings have already made spiritual progress beyond humanity's. In Lewis' space trilogy, it is because those worlds never experienced a fall into sin of the sort that Earth did. There are (despite what is sometimes claimed) a wide variety of ways that Christians can integrate the existence of extraterrestrial intelligence into their theologies. It may involve changes to the way that the person of Jesus, the idea of incarnation, and/or the means of salvation are conceptualized. But theology is not static, and it is only because some have managed to persuade themselves and/or others otherwise, that the possibility of Christians changing their minds or articulating new viewpoints is viewed as an abandonment of Christian theology on their part, rather than merely another exploratory task that Christian theology might find itself needing to engage in.

For some theologies, the biggest concern is not with the need for evangelism, but with the religious ideas that aliens will already have at the time we first encounter them. What would the implications be for a human theological system if a group of aliens also has precisely that system independently of us? What if the universe is full of religions that all agree with the views of one of your own tradition's terrestrial competitors? Alternatively, what might the implications seem to be if an entire planet never developed a concept of God or religion at all? Which would seem more challenging to one's own belief system? On the one hand, alien agreement with one's views might suggest the universality of truth and be understood to provide confirmation for one's own beliefs. On the other hand, it might seem to undermine the uniqueness of one's claim to know the truth, especially if that had been couched in exclusive terms which suggest that one's own group has truth that others do not.

That humans' gods resembled even the physical appearances of those who made and worshiped them is not a new observation. As humans encounter other sentient beings, new possibilities would arise in terms of how we think about what it means to be created "in the image of God." As we encountered ideas that are either much like our own or radically different, we would have new data that would undoubtedly be useful in exploring the role of biology in religious belief and experience. How much of our theology is shaped by our genetic heritage and our distinctive terrestrial experience? While some might find the questions frightening, because they mistakenly believe that theology offers timeless and unchanging truths, those who better understand what theology is and does should find any such new data exciting, and the prospect that it might provide answers to important questions exhilarating, even though those answers might not favor our own preferences. Theology itself has a long history not only of affirming human desires and the belief that we know the truth, but also of challenging us to sacrifice our own interest for the benefit of others, and calling us to humbly recognize that our own thinking and words can never be more than a pointer in the direction of the mystery and transcendence of God.

TIME TRAVEL

In science fiction, one can tell stories about the distant past or distant future without appealing to time travel. But positing the possibility of time travel allows the future and/or the past to impinge upon the present, and vice versa, in other ways. We have already mentioned the possibility of a

47

closed causal loop which involves our universe coming into existence in the past as a result of actions within our universe in the future. But aside from such large scale cosmic paradoxes, time travel stories allow for an exploration of both causality and of faith that focuses in on specific times and places. If you had a time machine, and could travel back in time to see if Jesus actually rose from the dead, would it be a good idea to do so? Obviously one concern is that your time machine's arrival might distort time and space, pulling Jesus into another plane of existence, while your arrival might be perceived as an angel announcing the resurrection. But apart from concerns about causing the events one went to observe, there is also the question of whether it is even appropriate to substitute knowledge for faith. Some would say that it is not, because they understand "faith" to involve belief without evidence. However, that is not the only possible definition of religious faith, and indeed, it involves understanding "faith" in a manner that places it at odds with science and history (and thus perhaps also with science fiction). Paul Tillich is one of many theologians to have made a convincing case that it is inappropriate to appeal to "faith" on matters that ought to be settled through the study of history, or science, or if possible, through time travel.[8]

What happens if your trip to the past does not confirm your beliefs? What if you travel back to watch the resurrection, and instead see someone steal Jesus' body? The science fictional possibility for travel through time and space makes for a nice thought experiment, when coupled with the question of what it would take to change your beliefs, or lose your faith altogether. If finding that Jesus, or Muhammad, or the Buddha, was not the person later stories claimed, ought it not to change your views? Would it be

8. See Tillich, *Dynamics of Faith*.

appropriate to stick dogmatically to beliefs despite seeing things with one's own eyes? Or ought one to try to explain away the problem by arguing that time travel might take one to a parallel universe where things were different? Wouldn't the existence of parallel universes with slightly or even very different Jesuses also raise serious issues for your worldview? And once time travel is possible, how could we rule out the possibility that competing fundamentalists will travel back, determined to prove or disprove particular views, and ready to resort to interference in history in order to make sure Jesus does indeed return to life, or to try to prevent him from ever being born in the first place? Many stories along these lines have been told, and many more will undoubtedly be written in the future. What they share in common is the use of sci-fi technology to examine the nature of faith and religious beliefs.

The main alternative to understanding faith as belief without evidence, or in spite of evidence to the contrary, is belief as trust, or as the ultimate focus that one's life is oriented around. If one's faith is not about dogmatically be-lieving what one chooses to or has been told to, but seeking wholeheartedly after truth and knowledge of God, then the willingness to investigate religious claims (with or without a time machine), and to change one's beliefs in light of the evidence, would not represent a loss of faith. Indeed, it can be an expression of faith, indicating the seriousness with which one takes God and truth. Depending on how one defines "faith," a time machine might threaten it, or provide an opportunity to express it, and correct and expand one's beliefs in the process.

QUESTIONS FOR REFLECTION

- If you had a time machine, where might you go, if you could go to any place or time of your choice? What if anything that you saw there could cause you to change your beliefs or even lose your faith? And if your answer is "nothing," what does that say about your viewpoint?

- If a powerful being from another world visited Earth, or you encountered it when exploring outer space, what characteristics would it need to have for you to consider it a god?

4

THEOLOGY AGAINST SCIENCE FICTION AND AS SCIENCE FICTION

IF THERE HAVE BEEN science fiction authors who were happy to caricature and denigrate religion, the latter has at times been happy to return the favor. While one can find authors in just about every tradition who have been happy to try to use popular films as a hook to talk about their own religious ideas, there have also been those who have denounced the entire genre as nothing short of satanic, encouraging people to believe in flying saucers, and to take an interest in their pilots who, according to these authors, are deceitful demons.

Ironically, even as some have denigrated science fiction, others in the same tradition have *written* science fiction. One can think, for example, of the likes of C. S. Lewis, whose *Space Trilogy* explored the idea that every planet has a spiritual overseer, and that Earth was the only planet that experienced a rebellion and fall of its inhabitants into sin. Such theological science fiction provides evidence of the potential for science fiction to serve as a means for an author to explore theological possibilities, to update ideas (or at least they way they are communicated) for a scientific era, and to teach their theology to others. But one can also consider the pulp novels in the *Left Behind* series an example of Christian science fiction. They claim to be an interpretation of the Book of Revelation, and yet bear greater resemblance to standard sci-fi tropes than to John of Patmos's critique of emperor worship.[1] Mysterious unexplained phenomena, mind control, global conspiracy, and other things that are part of modern end times/apocalyptic fiction, also very clearly belong to the realm of science fiction, and it is arguable that they are closer to that modern genre than to the ancient Jewish and Christian genre of apocalyptic literature. Ancient apocalyptic envisaged God bringing history to a close in order to judge humankind and establish the kingdom of God. Modern apocalyptic— even religious versions thereof—tends to include things like nuclear missiles or asteroids, sometimes even reading such modern things back into the Bible's imagery. We can even find the aforementioned sci-fi tropes in books which purport to offer biblical exegesis rather than a fictional narrative. However, when the Book of Revelation's locusts are turned into helicopters and its falling stars into ballistic missiles, one is not doing exegesis, but using ancient apocalyptic imagery as a source of inspiration for one's own sci-fi composition. There is nothing wrong with that, so long as it is acknowledged. The problem is that often this science fiction is mistaken for, or even deliberately mislabeled as, something else. As such, the relationship between biblical

1. See also Wetmore, *Theology of Battlestar Galactica*, 5.

and modern apocalyptic, between religious and secular sci-fi apocalypses, deserves a closer look.

APOCALYPTIC AND THE END OF THE WORLD

Terms like "apocalyptic" and "Armageddon" occur frequently in science fiction, often with no intended allusion to the genre of ancient Jewish and Christian literature that gave us these terms. Yet those terms do have specific biblical connections. "Apocalyptic" comes from a Greek word meaning "unveiling," disclosure," or "revelation" and denotes a kind of literature which offers a prediction of the future, leading up to something that at least sounds like the end of history and the final judgment. "Armageddon" is a place name mentioned in Rev 16:16, thought to denote the mountain of Megiddo, in the vicinity of which a number of famous battles had been fought. One can regard many sci-fi stories in the apocalyptic and post-apocalyptic genres as secular and/or speculative equivalents of the longstanding religious fascination with "the end." Or one can view them, at least in some cases, as works in the same basic genre, no less theological in their treatment just because they incorporate scientific elements.

It must be noted, however, that the idea that history must have an end is not one that has been universal either among religions or in the sciences. It seems safe to say, from the perspective of today's science, that the Earth cannot last forever, since eventually our sun will die in a process that will burn up the Earth along with it. But can humanity survive that process, as long as we find a "new earth" with a "new sky" where our existence can continue? Sci-fi has depicted it so often that it seems not just possible but inevitable. Yet despite the number of times we have read about it and seen it on screen, the hurdles involved in finding a world that would support human life and getting there are significant. Even if we can accomplish that, the problem of the ultimate fate of our universe remains. If the universe itself is destined to end (a question that scientists continue to investigate and debate), is there any way that our distant descendants could hope to survive that?

These are questions about the very distant future, and the survival of our very distant descendants, beyond the horizon of certain catastrophes that we can already see coming a long way off. Questions about whether we might survive those hurdles are speculative, and long before they become practical issues, there are other things we might face in the shorter term that could render such questions moot. Earth might be hit by an asteroid large enough to drive us to extinction. Humans might destroy ourselves and other living things through nuclear war, or by treating the environment callously. These issues already face us, and presumably will continue to be pressing concerns. We should consider whether, if we cannot find ways of living in peace, and using our resources wisely, it would be a good thing for us to colonize other worlds, or figure out how to escape the collapse or heat death of our universe by exiting it and entering another.

We shall return to a number of those points in our chapter on ethics. But there are plenty of scenarios that could bring human history to an end that would not be a result of our own action or failure to act. From natural phenomena such as solar flares or space debris, to unexpected consequences of well-intentioned research, to artificial intelligences rising up and seeking to kill their creators, to alien invaders (whether sentient or microbial illnesses), there are many ways that humanity has met its end, or risked meeting its end, in science fiction. If nothing else, such stories raise issues about ideas like divine providence, in a manner that goes beyond stories of more mundane, non-fictional forms of human suffering. They also raise questions about the value of our existence not only as individuals but collectively. Does humanity have to survive into the future for our existence to have been meaningful? Does the universe need to foster our survival as a species for it to seem plausible that a benevolent Creator brought it into existence?

If science fiction has offered secular stories of the end, modern religion has sometimes borrowed from science fiction, purporting to offer a vision of the future that derives from the Book of Revelation, and yet incorporating details which are classic sci-fi tropes. For instance, one could be forgiven for expecting Mulder and Scully from the *X-Files* to show up at some point in the *Left Behind* series, trying to figure out what is going on in this future of unexplained occurrences and global conspiracy. If science fiction has at times demonized religious believers, the sentiment has been reciprocated when some religious believers have suggested that encounters with aliens and UFOs are in fact encounters with demons. It is easy to scoff at the suggestion. But what, if anything, makes the religious suggestion that aliens are actually demons more laughable than the science fiction suggestion that demons are actually aliens? Once again, if such entities existed, would it matter what they are called? What would make either perspective on them fundamentally correct or incorrect? Often it is merely assumed rather than demonstrated that offering a scientific explanation for something disproves religious claims about it, or that conversely, offering a religious interpretation of something means removing it from the realm of what science can study.

Whatever may happen to our species, many consider the fate of individuals to be a more pressing concern, whether personally or theologically. Some religious believers are of the view that, without an afterlife, human existence is meaningless. That opinion is not a universal one in the realm of religion, although in some circles religion and afterlife have become so intertwined that people find it hard to imagine the one without the other. Yet the Jewish Scriptures (which is the same as the Protestant Old Testament) are almost entirely lacking in any interest in an afterlife. The imagery of dry bones living may appear as a symbol of national restoration, but literal resurrection of the dead to be punished or rewarded and live forever appears only in the Book of Daniel, which scholars view as likely to be the latest work in the Jewish canon to be composed. Other texts, such as the Book of Job and Ecclesiastes, seem to explicitly reject the possibility of an afterlife of the sort that many today take for granted, or at least hope for. But for the most part, the Jewish Scriptures simply ignore the matter one way or the other.

Science fiction has offered a number of scenarios in which an afterlife becomes a possibility, whether by downloading one's consciousness into a computer, or replacing one's body with a new one (whether artificial or biological in character), or by positing that science will one day discover that some form of energy corresponding to the notion of a soul does indeed survive death. But there are other less obvious candidates for sci-fi equivalents of hope for an afterlife. If there are an infinite number of parallel universes, so that there is always a version of you existing somewhere, would that comfort you in the same way that hope for conscious ongoing existence would? If not, why not? As it happens, the issue of continuity confronts several of the science fiction scenarios previously mentioned. If you download your consciousness into a machine, is what survives in it you, or merely a copy of you? (The same issue arises if you step into a transporter aboard the Enterprise—is what arrives on the planet below you or a copy of you?) Perhaps if we could harness nanotechnology to replace our neurons one by one, slowly, over a long period of time, with indestructible artificial ones, then we could preserve continuity and so be confident that the resulting person is the same one that began the process. But the whole issue of continuity and personhood is a complex one, both for theology and for science. An additional issue arises, however, with respect to those theologies that emphasize an afterlife, when one considers these science fictional scenarios. Will religions that offer the promise of eternity lose their appeal if human life—in *this* life—can be extended indefinitely through medical or technological means?

If not existing forever makes individual lives meaningless, then would the same apply to the fate of our species as a whole, or of the universe as a whole? Does it matter that, unless we intervene so as to prevent ongoing evolution, our distant descendants will not be humans of the sort we are now? Is it the continuity of descent that is desirable, or the preservation of humanity as we now know it? If one day the cosmos will collapse in on itself in a big crunch, would that render the existence of our entire universe meaningless? If so, why? For some religious traditions, history is thought of in cyclical terms, captured well by the phrase that recurred through the rebooted *Battlestar Galactica* series, "All of this has happened before. All of this will happen again." One can use science fiction to imagine distant futures where our universe is dying, and one in which a big crunch is followed by a new big bang that repeats everything that happened in our own, perhaps with minor changes. Would that scenario be a reason to rejoice (a version of you will exist in the future), or a reason for dismay (the existence of future you, like the existence of parallel universe you, might have things better or worse, and might make better or worse choices than you do)? Sci-fi allows exploration of such questions, getting at an important issue that theologians have also wrestled with: The *kind* of future existence that is posited makes an enormous difference. Living forever inside a computer may not seem appealing, but to many, the vision of heaven as involving eternal harp-playing on clouds seems even less desirable.

FUNDAMENTALISTS OF THE FUTURE

Science fiction often moves issues from the present into space and/or into the future, in order to address them in a less direct manner—although the way such topics are handled is not always subtle. Religious fundamentalism is a frequent feature in stories, and just as is the case in real-world fundamentalisms on Earth, the emphases of imaginary future fundamentalists often revolve around the matters discussed in this book (i.e., dogmatic adherence to particular views about how things began and how things will end). Yet in broaching this topic, what we sometimes get are cartoonish caricatures of religious belief, rather than something typical or realistic. Extremists can seem like easy targets, whether in the real world or fiction of any sort. And yet even in real life, there are reasons why people are dogmatic about religion, or dogmatic in their opposition to religion. It can be harder to challenge our demonization of others and explore realistic characters and their religious commitments in a nuanced manner, to dig beneath the surface and try to understand underlying causes and motivations of the views and attitudes we reject.

Looking at the theology of religious characters in science fiction often provides a good indication of whether the treatment aims at being sincere and sympathetic, or is itself dogmatic and dismissive. The rebooted *Battlestar Galactica* did a good job of getting us to join with humans in hating and fearing Cylons, as "toasters" that can be dismissed as mere machines, only to have the question of who is human and who is machine be blurred, the religious commitments of both receive both dogmatic and nuanced expression, and ultimately the story of both become inextricably intertwined in new ways. The TV show *Lost* did a good job of presenting both the danger of being too willing to believe and the problem of being too unwilling, with each perspective grasping part of the truth and missing part, and with even those who sought to grasp both perspectives failing to see the whole or solve all mysteries. And in the *Star Wars* films, we saw the Jedi good-guys at times being dogmatic, and a Sith lord insisting that such narrowness is not the way to "understand the great mystery." Extremes of narrowness and of openness both have their problems, and as we have already seen earlier in the present volume, one possible interpretation of *Star Wars* is that it advocates balance between the two opposing extremes. While science fiction always addresses the present, if we cannot envisage religious debates in the future or on other worlds that have the nuance and depth of those in the real world, never mind ones that are significantly different from our own experience, it reflects a lack of theological imagination. For if there is one thing that the study of theology reveals, it is that theology is always changing and developing.

MIRACLES AND CINEMATIC MAGIC

Conservative religionists tend to reject any theology that disagrees with their own. The truth of the matter is that a notion like the Force in *Star Wars* would meet with opposition in such circles, regardless of whether it was couched in the context of science fiction or not. Those who did not oppose it would seek to turn it into a Gospel illustration. On the other hand, the cinematic setting of the Jedi religion could make it seem particularly threatening, precisely because the movies do not merely suggest that there is a spiritual power which can move mountains, but depicts it being used to raise an X-Wing from a swamp, in a way that no religious practitioner today has experienced in real life as a power offered by their own faith tradition. Cinematic realism offers a significant challenge to religions, because however faithfully or with whatever liberties stories from the Bible are presented, the special effects look very similar, and it all serves to situate ancient stories of miracles alongside modern stories of the fantastic. If seemingly miraculous occurrences are depicted as having a scientific explanation, then that may seem to undercut religion's value—assuming that one understands the value of religion to consist of its success in providing something supernatural. If astounding events are depicted as mystical and mysterious in character, it still raises the question of the genres of all the stories in question, whether they are all more fundamentally similar to or different from one another, and the appropriateness of certain kinds of expectations and hopes in the real world we live in.

In fact, however, these reflections could lead us to the conclusion that the value of mythic stories lies elsewhere than in the veracity of their miracle accounts—a point that has been made by many, quite independently of science fiction, but which can also be made in relation to it. When significant numbers of people choose to put down "Jedi" as their religion on a census, something very interesting is happening. While few if any such individuals are likely to have a formal affiliation with a Jedi church, they clearly feel more affinity to a fictional religion from science fiction than they do for existing real-world denominations. The religion of the Jedi, to be sure, appears more effective on the cinematic screen than everyday religion does. But any fans who have tried using a Jedi mind trick to get out of a traffic ticket will know that the stories cannot be taken literally. So why do Jedi consider this religion more appealing, despite its stories not being factual, than other religions which they may have rejected precisely because they became convinced that their stories are not factual?

In both science fiction and religious literature, we encounter a range of voices and perspectives, including on theological topics. Some stories have mystical forces present and observable. And of those that do, some explain them away in terms of technology or trickery, while others leave room for the mysterious and unexplained. Some have characters with religious belief, yet no clear miracles or theophanies (appearances of God) that serve to confirm the truth of particular beliefs, which might eliminate the need for faith and the element of mystery. These differences, whether found in science fiction narratives or religious treatises, represent the articulation of different theological perspectives, emphasizing the divine presence and revelation, or the divine hiddenness and perceived absence. God in the monotheistic sense, it has been noted, rarely shows up in science fiction stories. But in many respects this is truer to the experience of real life than are many stories from ancient times, filled with voices from heaven and miracles galore, and for that reason requiring either unquestioning belief, or significant suspension of disbelief, on the part of most modern readers.

Sometimes the theological perspectives of science fiction authors, and thus also of their characters, do not reflect any depth of theological research or reflection on the part of the author. But in other cases, the theology is robust.

Sometimes a particular theological system lends itself naturally to expression in and through science fiction. The Latter-Day Saints, for instance, have incorporated belief in the existence of many inhabited worlds into their theology. It is not surprising, then, that Mormon authors have produced a number of significant works of science fiction. L. Ron Hubbard was a science fiction author before he became the founder of the Church of Scientology, and the teachings of that religion could be said to have a science fictional character to them as well.

If religions can have elements that resemble sci-fi, the reverse can also be true. When fans of a particular set of stories guide their lives according to values embedded in them, going so far as to make pilgrimages to conventions wearing special (if not indeed sacred garments), this deserves to be defined as a quasi-religious phenomenon. Perhaps one reason why theology has at times been hostile towards science fiction fandom is that it sees it as a competitor encroaching onto its own turf. If so, then an obvious follow-up question to ask is what is involved in offering one's own theology through the means of science fiction. After all, if the bringing of fictional religions to life on screen can seem threatening to real world belief systems, then the use of sci-fi storytelling to express one's theology, or to make an analogy to one's own practices, might just possibly provide a bridge that helps sci-fi fans understand and appreciate it. But just as the treatment of fundamentalism as violent and dangerous in sci-fi stories can offer merely flat stereotypes, with little depth or substance to the criticisms, theological science fiction faces the risk of coming across as too heavy handed. When the right balance between giving expression to one's theology on the one hand, and subtlety on the other, is found, the result can be very engaging. Often it will be necessary for someone to explicitly point out to a reader that an author is a Mormon, or a Baptist, or Jewish, and that certain ideas from those traditions are embedded in the story. When that happens, often the next step will be to look into the religious tradition in question, looking for still more connections. At that point, can one not say that one has done for science fiction fans much what Paul the apostle is depicted as having done for Greek philosophers at the Areopagus in Athens in Acts 17?

If theological ideas can be promoted effectively in science fiction stories, that can make for a more fruitful engagement between the two domains. Rather than merely defending against perceived attacks from others, offered by others through their science fiction stories, religious believers can use the genre to make their own positive case. This requires, however, that the religious ideas themselves be related to the future, to other worlds, and/or to developments in technology. If a tradition is unwilling to do that, then science fiction will always seem like a hostile and desolate environment. But that sort of engagement with the present, looking ahead to the future, is precisely what the historic apologists for religions (as opposed to the superficial modern internet versions of apologists) have done time and time again.

The treatment of living religions presents challenges for science fiction, as it does for all authors. Few today will be upset if the goddess Athena is incorporated in a science fiction story that turns her into an alien and, in the process, plays fast and loose with what was said about her in ancient Greek literature. But if a time traveler meets Jesus, even if the experience is a positive one, and is told of in a story written by an author who is a Christian, there is a high probability that someone will take offense and try to boycott the book or movie. But those risks are the very risks involved in relating a faith tradition to anything new, whether in the real present or in the imagined future. Science fiction need not be seen as a riskier a terrain than any other. If it is done well, by engaging the future plausibly from the perspective of one's theology, one can actually support the viability of that theology for those living in the present, but who themselves have one eye on the future and where things are going.

What are some concrete examples of how theology can be expressed through science fiction stories? If we consider that subset of stories that involve artificial intelligence, we still have more material than we can do justice to in a short volume like this one. Can robots be programmed to offer prayers and worship that would be pleasing to God? If not, why not? After all, how is that different from the way we teach and even indoctrinate biological children to do these things, offering prayers they have learned by heart long before they can fully understand the words that pass through their lips? Will bigotry stand in the way of the first time an android seeks ordination, or is considered as a candidate to be the pope? If someone programmed an artificial intelligence with St. Augustine's personality in order to teach seminarians, could that computer develop consciousness and deserve the last rights and a proper Catholic burial? These last couple of cases are not fictional examples, but allude to actual stories that have been written—"Good News From the Vatican" by Robert Silverberg and "Gus" by Jack McDevitt. They are examples representing a wider pool of stories that have been written, or could be written, on this one topic. It is hoped that this book may serve to inspire its readers not only to read existing stories, but also to write new ones.

There are many other ways that theology can be incorporated into science fiction in positive ways. There have been numerous yet very different stories told of worlds where the indigenous people seem to have no awareness of or capacity to sin, living in an extraterrestrial Eden. What happens when humans arrive there? Do they witness a "fall" or even contribute to bringing it about? Or what happens when a Christian space traveler shares her faith with a being from another world, in a manner that isn't merely regurgitating "four things God wants you to know" but an explanation of the beliefs and values that led her to act in the self-sacrificial manner that she did earlier in the story? Would it be an appropriate expression of Muslim faith, or an expression of inappropriate anthropocentrism, for a character to try to convert a being from another world to his own terrestrial tradition? Setting these questions in a science fictional realm has numerous benefits, allowing for contemporary issues to be broached in a less direct and thus less threatening manner, which does not only create the possibility for theological ideas to be conveyed to those beyond the boundaries of a faith tradition, but also for those within it to be confronted with the puzzles and challenges that they must wrestle with if their theology is to evolve and adapt so as to survive in the future.

QUESTIONS

- Which science fiction authors present their theological ideas effectively and compellingly? Which have seemed too subtle or too heavy-handed?

- In what ways can science fiction fandom be considered a religious phenomenon, and in what ways is it different?

- Think of an example of a sympathetic and unsympathetic religious character in some science fiction

stories you know. Why do you think the author(s)
depicted the characters in question as they did, and
why do you think you react to them as you do?

5

THEOLOGY AND SCIENCE FICTION AT THE INTERSECTION WITH PHILOSOPHY AND ETHICS

SCIENCE FICTION IS PERHAPS best known for its non-human characters. Lots of different kinds of fiction has human characters, but it is typically science fiction that has aliens and androids. Religious literature likewise tends to include stories of encounters between human characters and other non-human beings, such as gods and angels. Both, in bringing these other entities into the picture, pose questions and explore mysteries related to what it means to be human. Who are we? Where do we come from? Why do we seem at once so much like other animals, so much like the divine being or beings that we envisage, and at times so very unlike the divine? Science fiction, like theology, intersects time and time again with philosophy and ethics. Whole volumes have been dedicated to one show's treatment of philosophy or ethics, and so once again we will have to be content to merely hint at the breadth and depth of topics that can be found down the many pathways that lead off from this particular juncture.

The question of whether an artificially-intelligent computer can have a soul is purely theoretical at present. Those who pose the question also in the process draw to our attention that we typically do not have a clear and precise idea of what we mean by a "soul" in the first place, or what it means for a human being in the present day in real life to have one. Thus, science fiction provides useful thought experiments on the basis of which to discuss not only ethical matters related to the future of technology, but also about human nature. Cloning has likewise been a popular topic in science fiction, one that has veered in recent years into science fact. Yet clones have existed for as long as human history can be traced, in the form of identical twins. Thus one does not need an evil scientist, or a transporter accident, to address many of the issues that come up in sci-fi books, TV, and movies. Identical twins already raise problems for the notion that "life begins at conception" with the implanting of a soul. If so, what happens when the zygote splits to become two developing human beings in the womb? Does only one of them get the soul? Is it shared between them? Or does this suggest that popular notions of what a "soul" is break down in the face of real life, as well as in the face of hypothetical science fiction scenarios?

The soul in our time is predominantly a religious idea, and is often adhered to as dogma in the face of scientific challenges. Yet the notion of the soul is simply an ancient way of approaching the question of what makes human beings alive and conscious, and where that consciousness may be thought to reside. If in our time most neuroscientists view consciousness as emerging from brain function, it still remains known as "the hard problem" in that field. Even if some older ideas may need to be jettisoned in the wake of advances in our scientific understanding, there is no reason in principle why religions that adhere to belief in an afterlife cannot view the patterns and information that make up human consciousness as surviving, in much the way that a quasi-substantial soul was thought to. Perhaps it is not coincidental that the language of being "saved" or "lost" gets applied to both computer data and the eternal fate of humans. There are issues that arise in relation to any way of thinking about the soul, and science fiction can be very helpful in exploring those issues.

There has long been a tendency to speak of "soulless machines." But why should machines be thought of in this way? We may explore this by considering two sci-fi technologies: the teleporter and the android. The most famous example of the first is the *Star Trek* transporter, but many science fiction franchises have something similar. The category of "android" has in its very name the connotation of being human-like. Androids may be programmed artificially, but there are also stories that feature androids into which a human mind is copied or downloaded. In the case of teleportation technology, a human person is turned into information that can be copied, transmitted, and reassembled elsewhere. An obvious question to ask is whether the soul—whatever one may mean by that—gets copied as well. If the soul is something spiritual, that would imply that the technology is capable of transmitting spirit as well as matter. If the soul is the information pattern, we are still left with a question about whether that which materializes at the other end of the process is the same person or merely a copy thereof. Indeed, on *Star Trek* a transporter accident did sometimes result in more than one copy of a person existing simultaneously, whether as their complete self or with some distribution of the personality between the two entities.

What one thinks about teleportation should influence what one thinks about androids. If a soul is spiritual but can be transferred using technology, then in copying a human mind into an android, why should the soul not be able to be transferred as well? If a mind is simply an emergent property of a brain, why should a "positronic brain" not be perfectly capable either of receiving a copy of a biological human brain, or of being programmed with or evolving a sentient "soul" of its own?

Questions about the nature of the "soul" or of consciousness are at the heart of one of the practical issues that science fiction can help us address: the question of rights and who or what ought to have them. If we ever succeed in making artificial intelligences, or they emerge spontaneously from our interconnected computers, what status will such entities have in relation to the law? We might assume that, since we created them, we have the right to turn them off and to tell them what to do. But in the case of the human beings that we create in our own image and likeness through sexual reproduction, parents do not have inviolable and unlimited rights over their children, at least according to the legislation in effect in most human societies. If a sentience exists in a machine, however it may have come to be there, should it not have rights? If a person copies their mind into a computer, does the computer still have the civil, property, and other rights that the original human being had? Could that computer get ordained? (We won't ask about baptism, which would likely cause a short circuit.) Would it be murder to switch a computer off if a human mind had been transferred into it? Ancient sacred texts do not provide guidance about such matters, and science itself does not seem to be able to pronounce decisively on ethical matters. In science fiction, one can explore the issues and, in so doing, ask whether core principles of a religious tradition are or are not being applied.

Of course, it can be argued that a principle such as the Golden Rule does not provide a straightforward solution to these problems. That principle is understood to involve other *persons*, but it is the very issue of who or what a "person" is that is at stake in these discussions. How can one know whether a machine is a person, or is merely pretending to be a person, or programmed to fool us into believing it is sentient even though it is not? How can one determine whether a lifeform so different from us that communication or even mutual understanding seems impossible is nonetheless the kind of "other" that the Golden Rule applies to? Perhaps precisely because of this uncertainty, we ought to always, on principle, give alien and artificial others the benefit of the doubt. In human history, people have often found a loophole to moral teachings about other human beings by dehumanizing and demonizing individuals and even whole categories of people. We see the same done in science fictional realms in which intelligent machines are disparagingly referred to as "toasters" or "calamari," making it easier to pull the trigger.

The possibility of transferring a human mind into another copied body—whether a biological clone without a mind of its own, or an artificial android replica—also intersects with the hope of afterlife that many theological systems posit. We have already raised the question of whether the religious promise of eternal life, be it of a spiritual nature or in resurrected bodies on a new Earth, would seem as appealing and relevant in a world in which lifespans can be extended indefinitely, through more advanced medicine, life-extending drugs, artificial replacement body parts, or downloading of one's consciousness into a machine. Would longevity or immortality provided by scientific means be seen as the fulfilment of, or in competition with, what some religions offer? The impact would differ, depending on the religious tradition, since not all theological systems hope for an ongoing existence beyond death, and those that do often differ on the details. But we have not yet discussed the *ethical* issues related to these points. Could one legitimately make the case against using a treatment that prolongs human life indefinitely, simply by appealing to a biblical text that says "it is appointed for humans to die once" (Heb 9:27)? Certainly conservative approaches to theology and ethics, which cite prooftexts and consider a matter settled, might apply them to new technology in all sorts of different ways. Characters with such views regularly appear in sci-fi, often holding placards in front of the laboratory that has done the pioneering work. Others might insist that failing to prolong life where possible is in fact murder. Even for religious conservatives, different and competing prooftexts may be found. And even for more nuanced theological systems, which focus on broad principles, there will still be challenges in the face of new technologies, and sci-fi is both more useful and more interesting when it doesn't merely offer placard-holding protesters, but also people open to having their theology challenged by new advances, or to applying their principles in new and creative ways.

Science fiction can be useful for reflecting on the very nature of life—and life after death—itself. The soul has often been posited not only as the part of a person that survives death, but also that which provides continuity from the beginning through the entirety of their life. Of course, neurons might be said to provide continuity over the course of a normal human lifespan. But neurons consist of molecules, and not only can those molecules change even in cells that persist, but the molecules in your neurons may well have been part of someone else before they became part of you! It is hard to trace what exactly persists over long periods of time, and one approach to these matters—known as process theology—argues that looking for continuity of substance is misguided, and that we ought to be focusing our attention on events—which, of course, can take things from the past and carry them forward. These are challenging issues, about which whole books have been written. In short, if you wouldn't accept an offer to extend your life forever within the universe by scientific means, whether because of concerns about boredom, or because you are convinced that the "you" that will exist a million years from now would not still be the "you" that you are now in any meaningful sense, then it is worth asking whether any religious form of afterlife you may hope for faces the same issues. Science fiction allows us to explore all the varied scenarios that one can imagine in order to ask questions like who, what, and where "I" am, and what, if anything, makes me a continuous entity over time. Brain transplants, teleportation, dematerialization and rematerialization, cloning, duplication, transmutation, and possession or parasitical infestation—you name it, sci-fi has explored it. In the past, it was religious myths that explored these questions, telling stories of the gods (rather than imaginary technology) turning humans into animals, men into women and back again, so as to probe at key questions about personhood, gender, and other such subjects.

While some traditions hope for eternal life in connection with the immortality of the soul, the New Testament (as well as the Book of Daniel in the Hebrew Bible) speaks more often of the resurrection of the dead. Those who still think in terms of bodily resurrection usually do so in conjunction with belief in an immortal soul, which will simply become incarnate again in a new body. But others think of resurrection as a complete reconstitution of the individual who had ceased to exist after they died. This bypasses many of the problems that confront the idea of the soul—such as just what it is and how it interfaces with the body. But it brings new problems, and precisely the same ones that confront the person contemplating getting into a Starfleet transporter or similar teleportation device. Why should you think that the person that is reconstituted is *you* as opposed to merely being a *copy* of you? Would the copy have your rights, and own your property? What happens if a duplicate is accidentally created? Would you share your property—and perhaps even your marriage—with another you as a result? Would it be adultery for someone to have sex with the copy of their husband created by a transporter accident? What if a precise copy of you could be stored in digital form but (hopefully) only reconstituted after you died? Would it set your mind at ease about death, if you knew that an exact replica of you would exist again in the future? Why or why not? If your answer is yes, then perhaps all that is needed is an all-knowing God who knows your every thought, every detail of your form, to remember you for eternity? Or does a meaningful and desirable afterlife have to involve independent, continuous, personal existence to be considered eternal life *for you*? And does it have to be an *exact* duplicate of you? If not, then the idea that there may be parallel universes, or that the universe may be infinite, ought to provide us with some comfort, since in either scenario there will inevitably be other versions of you, and of your loved ones, that exist somewhere. Of course, some of them will have terrible experiences, and some of them will themselves be terrible people. Notions of infinity are impossible to wrap our minds around, but they come up as frequently in science fiction as in theology, and the puzzles each presents can be useful in exploring the other.

The issues we have discussed thus far have been focused primarily on the level of the individual. But sci-fi also explores ethical topics at the societal, planetary, and galactic levels. Many ethical issues present themselves in relation to subjects like space exploration—whether by us, or by others who may come to Earth before we manage to get very far beyond it. Stories involving humanity being conquered by aliens reflect our own human history of colonialism, the fear that others might do to us as we have done at times to one another. Often colonial powers have drawn the conclusion that the conquered lack souls altogether, or that, being presumed inferior in any number of ways, it is perfectly moral for the more advanced society to conquer them. To the extent that most people recognize that possessing superior technology does not mean that one has a superior culture or superior morals—and science has shown that human beings are more similar than different across the racial and ethnic divides at work in colonial situations—we presume our own right to survive and resist conquest when flying saucers appear above Earth's major cities and threaten us. But what if the new arrivals are as much more intelligent than humans, as humans are in relation to cats or dogs. Would it not then be moral for the aliens to treat us as their pets? Laws against cruelty to animals might still apply. But disposing of your pet human might not be the sort of thing interstellar police bother with, and when reported, it might only result in a small fine. If the choice was to eliminate our beloved animals or witness the demise of our own species, would it not be moral to sacrifice the one for the sake of the other? If so, then arguably a much more advanced society could sacrifice humans in the interest of their own survival. Science fiction raises practical questions about the rights that we think we deserve, and the rights we afford to others, including other living things on this planet.

These questions can be asked in specifically theological ways, whether in terms of the application of the Golden Rule, or in relation to stories in which multiple divine and/or angelic beings may rule over and interact with humanity, and may treat humans callously on the basis of their superior power and knowledge.

The issues of colonialism are relevant not just to the rights of organisms, but also to the new worlds we discover and explore. Should we have the right to lay claim to worlds, provided they do not have sentient beings living on them currently? Or would it be immoral to do so because sentient beings might one day evolve from the living things on the planet in question? Ought we to consider it moral to terraform other worlds, making them habitable to us? Does it matter whether doing so is humanity's only hope for survival, or does our survival not justify our making a world less habitable for other beings who might also need it?

When we encounter other sentient organisms, we may or may not be able to understand one another. While Genesis depicts humans as created with the capacity for language, and God intervening to multiple languages at the Tower of Babel, this bit of satire poking fun at the Babylonians should not be mistaken for a historical account. Languages evolve over time, and reflect the inherent biological capacities for sound-making in the makeup of human beings. Even across our shared humanity, there are languages and scripts that we have not managed to decipher. Science fiction introduces universal translators or other such equipment—or merely has the whole galaxy speak English—in order to sidestep the likelihood that, if we encounter other sentient entities, it will be a long road to learn each other's languages, and if we discover remnants of a civilization that once existed but which no longer does, we may never figure out what their language meant.

If language will present challenges, so too will differing values. Could a society exist somewhere where the things that we consider murder, or infidelity, or theft, or rape, are viewed as perfectly acceptable? How could we ever find enough common ground to make interaction possible? Earlier, we mentioned extending the Golden Rule as generously as possible to other entities that we bring into existence or encounter in space. But is it reasonable to expect them to reciprocate? Just as they might conceivably have ideas about the divine that are totally unlike anything that humans have formulated thus far, so too they may have ideas about morality that are totally unlike anything that humans have come up with. While it may be reasonable to expect them to have *some* concept of morality, assuming that they are sentient and social beings, it is also reasonable to expect their concepts to be more different from any of our human ways of thinking about such matters, than our human ethical systems are from one another. Science fiction often simplifies things by having aliens be much like us in shape, size, and thinking, with a few interesting differences here or there. These stories work much better as parables of how we ought to interact among human theologies and cultures, than as realistic depictions of what we ought to realistically expect if and when we do make first contact with aliens.

We have spoken of the rights and values of organisms living on planets. But what if a planet itself is sentient, as Eywa appears to be in the movie *Avatar*, echoing the idea of Mother Earth. Do only individual organisms on a planet have a right to respect, or could a planet as well? Does the planet have to actually have a personality for such considerations to come into effect? If the inhabitants of a planet revere their planet as a god, that does not necessarily make it a divine entity. But as for the question of the planet's *sentience* or *personhood*, is that the same sort of situation or a different matter entirely? Is it any easier to determine whether an entity is sentient than whether it is divine, or do both matters always depend on the subjective view of another, who defines divinity and personhood in particular ways?

If our human experience teaches us anything, it is that religious beliefs will not themselves guarantee either that other organisms, or a whole planet, is treated in a particular way. Some who revere the Ganges river as a goddess for that reason believe that she can be trusted to carry away pollutants with her cleansing waters, while others have argued that revering the river ought to lead people not to pour pollutants into it in the first place. Even within the same theological framework, people find very different ways of applying their shared principles, symbols, texts, and convictions. Science fiction often reminds us of that, showing us both humans and aliens, with different religious and non-religious viewpoints, exploiting and befriending, harming and helping, across all the different ways of existence our stories can imagine. Science fiction and theology share in common that, although they can offer pat answers, and some think that is the point, others would say that they are much better at raising questions. Hopefully this chapter, with its many questions, illustrates this point well. While philosophy often seems an abstract and difficult domain to those who look at it from outside, often theology and science fiction, each on their own, provide an entrance point at which people feel they can join in the discussion of important issues. Mike Alsford puts this well, when he writes, "The genre of SF . . . has the capacity to permit everyone, irrespective of their educational background, access to debates, discussions and speculations about some of the biggest questions that concern the human race."[1] But those big questions also intersect with theological convictions about God and human nature. Bringing the two together is the best way to give these important topics the kind of treatment that they deserve.

QUESTIONS FOR REFLECTION

- Given the philosophical and theological questions we have raised in this chapter, would you use the transporter on a StarFleet vessel, or would you insist on flying in a shuttle instead?

- If aliens came to Earth that did not share our belief that sentient beings like humans are inherently worthy of dignity and respect and deserve to be afforded certain rights, how would you try to make the case? How might things you know from science fiction, theology, philosophy, and/or ethics help you make that case persuasively?

1. Alsford, *What If?* vii.

6

SCIENCE FICTION AND THEOLOGY IN DIALOGUE AND SYNTHESIS

OVER THE COURSE OF this small volume, we have sought to provide an overview of the different ways that theology and science fiction have interacted and can interact. There is obviously much more that can be said, not only on the topics we have covered, but also on others. It will be sufficient if this book has offered illustrations of the different kinds of interactions, overlaps, intersections, and conversations that theology and science fiction can have. But readers will recall that, in our introduction, we suggested that the ideal—as in Barbour's models of interaction between religion and science—is for theology and sci-fi to engage in conversation as equal partners, working towards integration. In the introduction, it may not have yet been clear what such integration might mean. In this final chapter, we seek to make that explicit.

From the perspective of Barbour's models, the problem with the superficial noticing of Christ figures, the two-dimensional fundamentalist characters, and the treatment of the latest film or television show merely as an illustration of what one already believes, is that this approach allows one particular voice or perspective to predominate at the expense of the other. Science fiction and theology share in common that they naturally explore and reflect on big questions, key moments, and ultimate mysteries. What makes us human? Where did everything come from? What awaits us in the future? What do we dare to hope for? Theology and science fiction also share in common that each naturally raises questions about the other. To the facile assertion that people deserve rights, sci-fi offers thought experiments that dare us to achieve greater clarity about what constitutes a "person." To the insistence that one God alone really exists, sci-fi offers us a meeting with Apollo. And when the characters in sci-fi insist that the gods they encounter aren't "really" gods, or that an android has no soul, theology asks what is meant by this, how it is known, and offers conceptual tools that are useful in addressing such issues. Theological science fiction challenges the overconfidence of some sci-fi and some theology that scientism or religious dogma has all the answers, or at least the ultimate and most important ones. Faith, doubt, and reason all intersect in theology and science fiction, albeit not typically in equal measure. But where a particular theological approach, or science fiction author, fails to maintain the balance between these three, the conversation with the other may help offer a counterbalancing perspective.

Although there can be religion—and thus presumably also theology—without God or gods, the latter are central to much religion. Science fiction and theology in cooperation can get at answers to the question "what is a god?" better than either is likely to on its own. A quest for God or gods is unlikely to be successful, it could be argued, unless one has at least some concept of what one is looking for. And if mystical theology emphasizes the ineffable character of ultimate reality, science fiction often brings human observers into contact with transcendent dimensions and other beings and phenomena that defy description. If science fiction rarely has an all-powerful deity appear on the page or the screen, that mirrors our real life experience. Theology is done, for the most part, without miraculous revelations of a sort that could answer all questions. And science fiction explores distant space and the deep past and future through speculation and not through sight. Both involve movements between the observable and the imagination, pondering not only what is but what might be and what we hope for.

Science fiction might be felt to challenge liberal forms of religion every bit as much as, if not more than, conservative ones. If for the latter, the idea that angels and demons are aliens seems unacceptable, liberal believers might scoff at the notion that such entities literally exist at all. Stories abound in both religion and science fiction that challenge the reader's skepticism in the face of the seemingly impossible. The one might appeal to the supernatural while the other emphatically denies it, positing instead an explanation that is couched in scientific (or at least scientific-sounding) language. Yet both ask about the limits of skepticism, and at what point it is appropriate to stop doubting and believe what one has experienced, even if one cannot explain it.

Ultimately it does not matter whether the dialogue between science fiction leads to integration. As in the case of interaction around religion and science, there will always be some eager to pursue integration, and some who will interact with the presumption that they have much to teach and nothing to learn from the other. Dialogue may in fact look more like debate, proceeding on the basis of suspicion or even hostility rather than an eagerness to learn from the other, much less a desire to achieve some sort of mutually-beneficial union. What matters most is that some form of dialogue occur, and that it continue. The science fiction authors who cannot envisage a future for theology, and the theologians who cannot situate their religion's teachings and practices in the future sci-fi imagines, are both refusing to be sufficiently imaginative. That religion will disappear completely seems as much wishful thinking as that it will remain unchanged. The conversation that theology and science fiction can have is one that they *must* have if they are to look towards the future in a way that produces a plausible vision. If the past is anything to go by, the unexpected and surprising future with include elements that fall within the purview of both theology and science fiction, and will also include elements that neither foresaw—but some elements that each may perhaps foresee, thanks to the help of the other.

A THEOLOGY INFORMED BY SCIENCE FICTION

While theology tends to focus on religious thought and ideas, many have emphasized that theory and practice—what we believe and what we do—are inseparable. Many theologians have emphasized that theology and action *should* be inseparable, and have resisted the attempt to focus on one to the exclusion of the other. We have seen this already, as our exploration of theology and science fiction has brought us time and again into contact with questions of ethics—of what it would or would not be appropriate to do in specific science fictional scenarios in light of particular theological teachings and convictions. In those explorations, we have seen that sci-fi sometimes leads us back to our terrestrial roots and traditions once more, and provides a vantage point from which to appreciate and apply them in new ways. In this section, we'll conclude our journey by returning not just to Earth, but to the Bible, and by taking a closer look at what it has to say about aliens.

LOVING THE ALIEN

The Bible actually has a great deal to say about the alien. True, the authors of the Pentateuch did not have Klingons or ET in mind. But our stories about encounters with extraterrestrial others are inspired by our encounters with terrestrial others, and often the stories have been written with the specific aim of seeking to broaden our perspective and provoke us to greater inclusiveness. Many texts about aliens in the Bible have the same aim. How frequently your Bible mentions the "alien" will depend which translation you read—the word is quite frequent in the New Revised Standard Version, for instance, but rare in the New International Version. But extraterrestrials can fit comfortably within the semantic range of words like "foreigner," too.

The alien is often rejected and kept at a distance, since the alien brings strange ideas and customs into our midst. We shall see below that the Bible's statements about the alien are not all positive and kind. But some are, and it is the choice of the interpreter where to focus attention and what if anything to seek to apply today. Leviticus 19:33–34 (NRSV) reads, "When an alien resides with you in your land, you shall not oppress the alien. The alien who resides with you shall be to you as the citizen among you; you shall love the alien as yourself, for you were aliens in the land of Egypt: I am the Lord your God." The Bible has a great many warnings about the potential impact of foreign people and practices on the Israelites' own faithfulness to their God. Yet in the midst of that, we find a command not to oppress the alien, nor to treat them differently, but to love the alien as oneself. To love one who is referred to as "neighbor" can be challenging enough. Many do not like science fiction precisely because they find the people dressed in costumes, which aim to depict what aliens from outer space might look like, to be grotesque and repulsive. But we find our fellow human beings to be disgusting and unbearable at times too. Often we go so far as to demonize other people. And science fiction has something to say about that. If the distinction between the alien and the god has been explored, so too has the distinction between the alien and the demon. There have been multiple stories about beings that at least resemble the historic depictions of demons by humans.[1] But ought we to judge by appearances? When we do, we are notorious for making poor decisions, and for unfairly mistreating others. Some great science fiction stories have seen humans quickly side with aliens who resemble us in a conflict with beings which appear not just unlike us but repulsive. Yet eventually it becomes clear that the latter are the ones that are the victims of injustice perpetrated by our fellow humanoids. The challenge, when it comes to loving the alien as the Bible teaches, is our tendency to view them as so very different from us that they are not even human, so that the teaching does not apply. Science fiction can help give the biblical challenge new poignancy, as it brings into the picture beings that clearly are not human, who look nothing like us, and yet may share our highest moral values and thus deserve our respect, even our love. Loving the alien—terrestrial or extraterrestrial—is not

1. *Childhood's End* by Arthur C. Clarke is a particularly good example, but so too is the episode "The Daemons" (S8/E5) from the television series *Doctor Who*.

easy, and deciding how to apply such teachings may not be simple. But science fiction can help keep us from avoiding the challenge of such teachings, or from finding seemingly simple ways of setting aside or dismissing such teachings, by presenting us with new and far more exotic aliens, and testing us to see whether we can apply our moral values even to them.

WELCOMING THE ALIEN

Our stories about aliens from outer space reflect our hopes and our fears, based on our encounters with other human beings, as well as our awareness of what we ourselves have done, or our country or society has done in the past. Some look to space hoping that other wiser beings might come and teach us. But would we really embrace alien wisdom that told us to love one another, when we have refused to accept such teachings either from our fellow human beings, or when they have been offered as purportedly divine revelations that come to us from above?

The biblical references to aliens are more dense in the Pentateuch than anywhere else in the Bible. And that is not surprising. There we have the stories of the Patriarchs arriving as aliens in the midst of the Canaanites and being at least tolerated, for the most part. There we also have the stories of the Israelites living as aliens in Egypt and finding themselves first influential, and then marginalized, and finally enslaved. We also find the stories that prepare for the narratives of invasion and genocide, in which the Israelites take the land of others, supposedly having been commanded to do so by God. We cannot ignore that this is the introduction to the biblical story of the alien, and that this is the disturbing context of its laws on this topic.

Loving others as a generic, abstract principle is something that many can assent to. But what about bringing those others into one's midst with all their strange practices and different ideas? Humans whose sacred traditions demand love for others have often been unwilling and/or unable to apply that teaching to those others whose sacred traditions are different from their own. Why does it so often seem easier to love someone who genuinely hates us personally, than to love someone who merely disagrees politely with our own religious ideas? Is this appropriate, or profoundly ironic, or perhaps both? Ought one to not merely love the stranger from a distance, but welcome them, their different values, and their different religions into one's midst?

The Bible is much more ambivalent on this last point. Aliens in the midst of ancient Israel were not required to observe Jewish festivals and food laws. But they did have to observe the Sabbath, and were to be punished if they blasphemed the name of Yahweh or offered their child to Molech (Lev 20:2; 24:16). The Israelites were warned against succumbing to the temptation to worship as their non-Israelite neighbors did. In Ezra 10, the Israelites are depicted as repenting of having married foreign women and divorcing them. These issues are not limited to the Bible by any means. Especially when it comes to smaller people groups and traditions, or groups which have moved to a new location where they are in the minority, there is often a desire to see marriage take place only within rather than beyond the bounds of the community, because intermarriage makes it unlikely that one's own ethnic, cultural, and/or religious identity will be passed down to the next generation. If rejection of the other can be xenophobic and hateful, is simply welcoming and even intermarrying with the other endangering to one's own group? If harming and endangering the existence of another group is wrong, isn't the same true if one endangers one's own?

Are there necessary and appropriate limits to the welcoming of the alien? Science fiction explores this too, and in a variety of ways. On the one hand, it depicts a wide variety of ways that humanity might meet its doom at the hand of aliens. Stories of giant craft coming to our skies recall our history of ships coming to a shore, and bringing with them new people who might conquer and rape, or merely settle and threaten to displace. We fear that others from space will do to us what we have previously done to our fellow human beings. Yet the challenge is to not simply do as has been done to us, perpetuating conquest and upheaval, but instead to do to others as we would want done to us. If science fiction has depicted humans responding with a quick resort to violence when patience would have revealed a better alternative, it has also depicted humans seeking to trust and negotiate only to find ourselves exploited and threatened. Many religious traditions teach that the outcomes of such scenarios do not determine what was appropriate. If we are committed to being welcoming, we may not altogether exclude the possibility of war or expulsion altogether, but we will treat them as very much a last resort, even if that means risking that our patient efforts at peaceful interaction may make us vulnerable. Both religious teachings and science fiction stories have asked us to reflect on this question repeatedly: if we must risk losing our lives or our values, which should be given priority?

JUSTICE FOR THE ALIEN

Exodus 12:49 emphasizes that there must be one law that applies to both Israelites and aliens in their midst (see also Lev 24:22 and Num 15:15–16). Doing unto others what we would want done to us, when adhered to in a rigid manner, can be oppressive. Sometimes those who are different from us do not want us to do to them *exactly* what we would want done to us. We might be delighted if aliens with advanced technology were to remove carbon monoxide from our air. But that doesn't mean that we ought to do the same on another planet, the inhabitants of which in fact breathe that which is poisonous to us, and would die if we were to make their atmosphere more like Earth's.

Few think that a rigid application of the Golden Rule is appropriate. The point, most would agree, is about empathy—about recognizing the subjective perspective of the other, and not simply doing to them that which they would not wish us to do, even though we might wish it if the roles were reversed. Science fiction can help us to grasp this point. In everyday settings, we are prone either to assume that because someone looks like us, their viewpoint and desires match our own, or conversely, that because they dress or speak differently from us, there is no shared basis for empathy. Science fiction tells stories in which the aliens we encounter may hold to values more radically different from that of viewers than any other human culture is, and yet in which the human characters find ways of empathizing and understanding nevertheless, and then act in ways that express that empathy in practical actions. Conversely, those who are aliens from the perspective of humans likewise show themselves capable of learning and understanding. As the epilogue to the movie *Terminator 2: Judgment Day* famously put it, "if a machine, a Terminator, can learn the value of human life, maybe we can too." We fear the other both because we lack empathy, and because we persuade ourselves that they lack empathy. Ironically, in so doing, we foster hatred even while we claim to be acting in love. Because, if there is a risk that we will speak of loving everyone in a manner so generic that it ceases to challenge us day by day, there is also a risk that we will allow our love for those closest to us to seem to justify our attacks on others, whom we rightly or wrongly perceive as a threat to our loved ones.

LEARNING THEOLOGY FROM THE ALIEN

Those who read the Bible without an awareness of the historical and literary context of the texts within it will most likely fail to notice the many points at which the alien has influenced it. Whatever one's view of the origins of the Israelites and their relationship to the societies usually referred to as Canaanite, there can be no denying that there is shared terminology (e.g., for things like kinds of sacrifices), a shared heritage of concepts and stories, of words and ideas. It is not thought to be a coincidence that it is in the era of interaction with the dualistic traditions of Persian religion that the Israelites developed apocalyptic literature, with its dualistic imagery. In the New Testament, we find authors and characters using terms like Logos borrowed from Greek philosophy, or actually quoting from poems about Zeus (as Paul is depicted doing in Acts 17). Whatever the *rhetoric* about the alien may be at points in the Bible, the *influence* of the alien can be seen clearly. The same remains true throughout religious history. Tertullian may have asked "What has Athens to do with Jerusalem?" and argued against encroachments of philosophy into Christianity (*De praescriptione haereticorum* 7). And yet we can see clearly (even if he could not) the way his own background in Stoic philosophy made it possible for him to articulate the concept of God's "Threeness" (Trinity) in the specific way that he did.

However much some might try to resist and reject the alien, the truth is that the alien is among us and within us, and in some contexts *is* us. Science (and not only science fiction) makes clear that there is no sharp delineation between the human and the non-human, between the atmosphere of Earth and space. If it turned out that the beginnings of life on Earth resulted from the arrival of organic materials from space (as some scientists as well as sci-fi authors have suggested), would that make us and other living things "alien intruders" on this planet? If other beings that evolved on the planet long before us had developed space travel technology and left, and were one day to return, would they have a right to reclaim their homeworld of origin from us? Such science fiction scenarios can help us to reflect on political and territorial matters in the real world. But they can also help us to problematize the very notion of the "alien."

Theologically speaking, from the standpoint of the Abrahamic religious traditions, the entire universe if God's creation. So, much as was said to the Israelites about the Promised Land, the entire cosmos belongs to God, and we are "but aliens and tenants." Augustine famously said that wherever truth is found, it belongs to God (*On Christian Doctrine* II.18.28). That presumably applies not only to humans like Plato, but to any extraterrestrial philosophers we become aware of in the future. One will find both within science fiction, and within the theological resources provided by a wide array of different traditions, a basis for welcoming alien persons, and for viewing their ideas as things which may legitimately be engaged with, evaluated, and perhaps even embraced. In an era in which the welcoming of terrestrial aliens is a pressing matter that is known to stir up controversy, it is encouraging to know that the combined resources provided by an integrated approach to theology and science fiction have the potential to help us combat xenophobia, and to challenge us to engage with contemporary as well as future issues in creative ways.

QUESTIONS FOR REFLECTION

- How straightforward is it to apply biblical references to "aliens" to the kind of aliens that science fiction envisages? Which verses fit well, and which do not? Is it even appropriate to apply the Bible in this way, simply by focusing on the word "alien"? What other texts or principles would be more appropriate to use?

- In light of the chapters you've read since we first argued the case, do you agree that the best approach to interaction between theology and science fiction is *integration*, trying not merely to relate the two but to merge them together in a way that preserves the strengths and insights of each? Are there particular kinds of stories or theological ideas that are particularly resistant to integration of this sort?

7

THREE THEOLOGICAL
SCIENCE FICTION
SHORT STORIES

WE HAVE MADE REFERENCE to numerous specific examples of science fiction laced with theology, and theology laced with sci-fi tropes and motifs. We have also indicated that there is plenty of room for more science fiction to be written, exploring old ideas in ways that are slightly different or very new, or breaking new ground and trying to imagine a future that is very different from any terrestrial reality, or a planet very different from Earth, as well as very different alien or future human theologies. Neither of the three very brief stories offered here does anything very radical. However, it nevertheless seemed fitting to conclude the volume by ceasing to merely talk about stories, and actually tell some. It is hoped that this volume as a whole will not only lead to interesting engagement with existing theology and science fiction, but also to the crafting of even more imaginative stories and theologies.

CERTAINTY

Intro to Luke

"I'm recording this so that you can be certain, as I am . . ."

Kelly Wallace pushed the button on the console again and stopped the recording. Before she finalized it, and recorded the concluding phrase, before she made it final and sent it off, she wanted to listen to the entire thing one more time. She wanted to be sure she got it right. Not that she actually wanted anyone to hear the recording. And not that anyone would believe her if they listened to it. Why should they? Even though her crew saw the same things she did, and even though none of them could ever waver in their certainty, having seen what transpired with their own eyes and heard with their own ears, why should anyone else listen to them or trust them? She would rather that everyone simply keep quiet. And maybe the others would. But these were hard things to keep to oneself. And if others talked about it, she wanted her perspective to be heard as well. After all, the destination had been her suggestion, and the research that got them there was in large part her own, however much it was a collaborative effort.

So she pressed play, and listened to the message again . . .

"This is Kelly Wallace. I'm recording this so that you can be certain—about what happened, about what I've seen, about why I've left, about everything.

I'm assuming that I don't need to do introductions. I am quite sure that there is no one anywhere in the world—at least, no one who would be interested in listening to this recording—who won't already know the background to it. The work I did first at Cornell, and then subsequently funded by an independent donor, on time travel. The successful tests, the ones you've read about in the news. The development of a working prototype time machine. The discussions about where to go. The decision, and the dematerialization of the machine with myself and a crew of others on board.

Presumably that's the last you heard?

For the record, the decision to go to first-century Jerusalem was as much my idea as anyone else's. I always wondered as a child what it would be like to witness it all—the life of Jesus, the crucifixion, the resurrection. As I moved from lukewarm faith into agnosticism in my teens and twenties, I still wondered—what would I have seen if I had been there?

I didn't get involved in time travel research to answer those questions. But once the initial phases of the research proved to be successful, and we started discussing where to go for our first major test, I knew where *I* wanted to go. It didn't take much effort to persuade the others, although I am sure you can imagine the debates that ensued about the details. Would it be appropriate to record what we saw? Could we do so without revealing that we were from the future and potentially changing history? Would it be unthinkable to go there and *not* record what we saw? Would anyone believe us if we said we saw the resurrection? Would anyone believe us if we said it was all a myth?

Already having had some exposure to the relevant languages in my undergrad years, I took intensive advanced courses in Biblical Hebrew, New Testament Greek, and most importantly, I sought to add Aramaic to the mix. The ancient Roman world was a place of many intersecting cultures, and so I was confident that a funny accent and imperfect grammar wouldn't give me away. But would I have enough vocabulary to find the right place? I studied hard, as quickly as I could, to make the most of our journey. What was the point of going if we managed to hear something important, but had no hope of understanding it?

Our first attempt to get there overshot the mark by more than a thousand years. We were close to the right place, off by merely a few hundred meters, but it was the wrong time by far. Yet I wasn't going to miss the chance to learn something where we had ended up, even if it had been by accident—after all, we were the first people from the future to visit that particular moment in history, and for all we knew we would be the only ones to ever do so. Our machine blended in as easily then as it would have if we had arrived in the right time, but I found some people to talk to much too quickly, and worried that our arrival might have been witnessed. The individuals I spoke with seemed to understand my Biblical Hebrew, although their accents and pronunciation were like nothing I had ever heard before, and there were plenty of unfamiliar words. It was a good thing that what I wanted to find out kept me firmly within the vocabulary I had learned. I wanted to know if they had heard the stories that I had learned in Sunday school, and studied in my Hebrew classes—stories of Abraham, Isaac, and Jacob, of Moses and the Exodus. They had not. I thanked them, apologized for having retained them, and was certain I offended them by refusing their offers of hospitality.

What had I learned from talking to them? What did it mean? Was ancient Israel a myth altogether? Or had I just happened across people who were among the many non-Israelite peoples in the land? Or was there another possibility that I was overlooking? It would have taken a much longer stay to find answers, and this time and place was less crucial to my curiosity than our originally-intended destination. I wanted certainty, one way or another, and this place didn't offer it.

We waited until there was no one in the vicinity as far as we could see, and then we departed, aiming once again for the first century, for the year 33 (which historians consider to most likely be the year of the crucifixion), for the site where the Church of the Holy Sepulcher would later stand. While it was possible that the location was not in fact where Jesus had been crucified and buried, historians I spoke with said the chances were very good. And presumably we could tell if that was the place or not once we got there. Soon I would know.

The place we arrived was pitch black. We were there merely to observe, and so we did not completely reenter the normal space-time continuum. We remained at the edges of normal existence, able to observe as though we were physically present, and yet we were not in any tangible way. The darkness suggested to me that we had the right place, the right time. We must be inside the tomb! Heat scans showed no signs of life. And so how would we see? How would I know what was happening? Would we be able to see a change on the heat sensors, if life returned to a corpse that was in the tomb just outside? Part of me began wondering whether this was a foolish undertaking. Part of me began wondering whether we should in fact simply materialize completely and turn on an exterior light.

But then something began to happen. I could see some kind of light inside the tomb—visible light, not a reading on a heat sensor. My heart began to pound with excitement. Was it an angel, or light from outside as grave robbers opened the tomb and prepared to steal the body? I honestly didn't care which it turned out to be, as long as I found out.

Then the time ship began to shake.

The scanners indicated a major distortion in the spacetime continuum. I checked the controls and there was nothing that our ship was doing that should have caused anything like that. Of course, we were new at this, and so there might have been any number of things that we failed to account for or expect. But that did not seem likely. The readings on our instruments were off the chart, of a magnitude that would have required thousands of spacetime ships all converging on the same location, the same precise spot in space and time.

And then it hit me. I wasn't the only one who wanted to know. Having found a way to travel through time, my work would enable others to travel as well. And so presumably there *were* thousands of others, converging on this space, eager to see, determined to know, and as a result, threatening to tear apart the very fabric of spacetime itself.

I would have to act fast—I barely had time to think consciously about what I was doing. I tried to pull our ship quickly into and then back out of ordinary spacetime, hoping to create a ripple that would jostle the other ships out of phase, and either bump them out to keep them from materializing simultaneously in this one point in space and time, or at least get them to realize that they were in danger of doing damage not just to a historical moment, but to the very fabric of the universe.

The shaking did not stop. So I tried something else.

I sent a message, broadcasting across all standard frequencies as well as on external speakers. "You are too late. He is not here. He has already risen. You can see the place where they laid him. But if you all converge on this spot, you will risk destroying not only yourselves and your ships but this place and this moment that is so important to you. There are too many ships trying to converge on this same tiny spot. Go to Galilee—there you should be able to see him."

The shaking seemed to grow less intense, but did not stop entirely. Was anything I was doing having any effect? Perhaps the spacetime distortions prevented some or all of the message from being received. Maybe the other ships had heard the message, but their determination to see and know was clouding their judgment.

The light in the tomb grew brighter, and I realized that it was most likely neither an angel, nor someone opening the tomb, but a breach in the fabric of space and time itself.

There was nothing more that I could do to try to prevent what was happening. We had to save ourselves. I moved the controls and withdrew our ship from the space-time continuum.

And suddenly there he was in in our midst. A man was standing there, naked, inside the ship. A man with scars on his wrists and his ankles.

I was shocked when he spoke to me in English.

"Kelly," he said, "your presence here today made history. You came merely to see, but your work created a way for others to come too, and together you made a tunnel leading outside of space and time, a bridge to a reality beyond this one, beyond even the one in which your ship now exists outside of normal space and time. I was pulled into it, and now exist there, even though I can be here as well, and everywhere else. Thank you, for the role you have played, and for what you have made possible."

I was stunned. What did this mean? I asked him, "Are you saying that *I* caused the resurrection?"

"You were involved in the process, if that is what you are asking," Jesus replied.

"So what does this mean?" I asked him. But he just smiled at me, raised his hand in what could have been construed as a blessing or merely a wave goodbye, and then he vanished.

I had so many questions in that moment. I still have them, and many more besides. Did God send me to that moment to participate in the resurrection? Was it foreordained that I would do that? Could I have done otherwise? Was it inevitable that *someone* would do it? Or was there no God who was a part of this, and it was just me, traveling through time, asking about stories and planting the seed of them in the minds of people, visiting a tomb and causing a resurrection, and bringing about the faith that would then be taught to me, in a bizarre causal loop that made no logical sense?

Perhaps I should be satisfied. I had seen what I came looking for with my own eyes. Jesus rose from the dead, not merely in the sense of a corpse returning to life, but an entering into a new kind of existence unlike anything any human being had experienced. It was what the theologians had said all along.

Yet I hadn't just seen it. I had *caused* it. And I didn't know what that implied. Did that indicate that there *is* a God, who orchestrated these things to raise his chosen one from the dead? Or did it indicate that there isn't a God, and that humans are the cause even of things that seem miraculous to us? Is the technology I invented going to be the reason that people believe in gods and miracles, inspiring future humans to travel back, looking for gods and angels that are in fact us, time travelers from the future?

I told you at the beginning that I am certain. I know exactly what happened on that day, in that tomb, to that person who was once dead, and who now lives forever more. I am certain, and yet I have more questions as a result of this new certainty.

I won't return to my own time for good. I cannot stay here, having seen and experienced these things. I will probably go to the future, to find out what stories people are telling a long time from now about these things that happened. What stories they are telling about me. What happens to Christian faith in the future as a result of the things that I did, and the stories people tell about it. Maybe I will find that the stories bear no resemblance to the truth. If I try to put things right, will anyone believe me? Can any person's testimony overcome the beliefs that people find themselves with?

I may one day know the answers to those questions. But before I go, I need to leave this message, so that others can hear my story, and believe what they will about it.

My name is Kelly Wallace. I witnessed the resurrection with my own eyes, and now I am certain about things that no one before me was ever this certain about. And I want to make sure you know what I now know. I'm recording this so that you can be certain, as I am, if you want to be.

But you should know this: Certainty is not all it is cracked up to be. Certainty sucks."

[END MESSAGE]

I TOLD YOU SO . . .

The day had finally arrived, and Gen. Forrester breathed a sigh that was at once one of relief and of anxious anticipation. Their contact with the Yorok, the first extraterrestrial race of whose existence Earth had come to have definitive proof, had begun several decades earlier, when a team of radio astronomers had accidentally intercepted a message from a Yorok exploration team that was doing research in the Epsilon Eridani system. The message, which remained indecipherable, nevertheless was clearly not of terrestrial origin nor produced by a natural phenomenon, and a message sent back by the scientists on the same frequency managed to be detected by the Yorok while they were still in the vicinity (broadly speaking, of course) of our solar system.

The events that followed were well known, but Forrester could not help reviewing them in his mind as he stood there at the designated landing site. Messages had been sent back and forth—in English, as the Yorok proved much more adept at deciphering and learning this human language than American scientists and linguists were at making sense of the language of the Yorok. Their race's planet of origin was in a star system that no longer exists, apart from the stunning gas clouds that were left after their star went supernova. They had now spread to many natural and artificial worlds, at distances of tens and even many hundreds of light years from their original home. This wandering had brought them within the vicinity of earth, a planet whose radio-wave emission was clearly detectable even at a distance of some several light years, and it was this that led the Yorok to send a signal in our direction.

This was the story as the Yorok told it, and Gen. Forrester had no real reason to doubt it and no alternative story to put in its place. But today, on the day when the Yorok ship was scheduled to arrive for Earth's first face-to-face contact with an intelligent non-terrestrial race, he felt ill at ease. "If they came here looking for places to live," Forrester thought to himself, "Earth would be an obvious choice. All they would need to do is clear it of its present inhabitants." A hall had been prepared for the beginning of face-to-face diplomatic relations once the Yorok ship arrived. Large numbers of high-tech weapons were also prepared both on the ground and in orbit, in case the Yorok should prove to be less friendly in person than they had been in their radio communications. And so Gen. Forrester waited for the ship to arrive. They had been tracking it since it entered the solar system, of course, and the Yorok ship exactly matched the description that had been radioed to earth, and had precisely followed the course that had been mutually agreed upon. Everything was going right on schedule. But that didn't mean that there could not be surprises of a sinister nature in store. And so Gen. Forrester waited for the ship to arrive, ready to be friendly and welcoming, ready to retaliate at any sign of hostility.

In the end, Gen. Forrester was finally able to breathe a sigh that was one purely of relief. The Yorok ship landed, its crew of seventeen disembarked, and once they entered the building Forrester felt that the likelihood of any less-than-friendly action on the part of the Yorok was highly unlikely. They were unarmed, as far as anyone could see, whereas US soldiers lined the entrance corridor to the meeting hall, ready to intervene at a moment's notice. The Yorok looked so much like what someone who grew up watching science fiction might have expected, that Gen. Forrester was sure he was not the only one who half expected that at any moment they would pull off their masks and turn out to be human actors engaged in an elaborate publicity stunt. They took their seats (specially designed to suit their anatomy—it was a good thing the scientists had thought to ask about that!), face to face with leaders and representatives from a number of different nations, plus scientists and a number of individuals whose identity Forrester had been told he did not need to know. Cameras were set up all around the hall, and a carefully-vetted film crew was actively but unobtrusively making sure that this historic event would be recorded for posterity, as well as for careful study and analysis.

The vice president of the United States, Joel Greenberg, led the meeting—the Yorok had said they did not have anyone who was of a sufficient rank among their people to engage appropriately in diplomatic relations with a national leader, and the government had quickly picked up on this and used it as an excuse to keep the president away from the initial proceedings. Why put the leader of our country's life on the line until it was much clearer what intentions the Yorok had? "On behalf of the United States of America," Vice President Greenberg began, "and of the entire human race, let me welcome you to our planet, and tell you how happy and excited we are that you are here with us today".

"Thank you," replied the captain of the Yorok research team, who had managed to learn quite fluent English through his interaction via radio with scientists on earth, and through language-learning materials that had been transmitted in anticipation of this meeting. "We are happy to be here. Wish you that we shall begin now, or wish you that we wait for the other races to arrive?"

Greenberg looked nervously at Gen. Forrester, who had taken his place standing near the table, where he could make eye-contact with the vice president and thus communicate if necessary. "Other races?" he asked.

The Yorok spoke among themselves for a few moments in their own language, making facial expressions that none of the humans present knew how to interpret. Then the Yorok team's leader turned back to Vice President Greenberg and said, "We were led to believe that this planet is inhabited by many races, each with their own language and nation."

Greenberg smiled with relief, as some chatter coupled with nervous laughter began to spread among the humans present. "The earth is inhabited by many people-groups, each with their own culture, language and nation, but all of them are humans," he explained to the Yorok.

The Yorok spoke among themselves for a few moments again, then the Yorok leader spoke again to the humans present. "I understand. In our distant past we had a situation similar to this one, which is now on your planet."

"So are we to understand that now your entire planet is united as one?" asked a human anthropologist who was present.

"Not only our planet. Our race, the Yorok, is united, even though today we live on many planets," one of the other Yorok now explained, showing that he/she/it too had mastered English.

"Do you mean to say that the Yorok have no wars among themselves?" interjected Gen. Forrester, at once surprised and somewhat suspicious of what seemed an implausible claim, one that might simply be a ploy to lure the inhabitants of earth into a false sense of security.

"The Yorok have not been involved in conflicts of this sort for many thousands of years," explained the ship's captain. "Nor do we engage in conflict with any other races. Our ships and their crew have equipment that might be considered weapons, but only for use in blasting away space debris, and for self-defence against wildlife on exploratory missions on worlds not inhabited by intelligent life forms."

"That is quite impressive. I think we will have a lot to learn from your people," said one of the scientists present. "Is there any advice you could give us briefly as to how you manage to avoid conflicts, or could you tell us something of the history of your people and the way it learned to overcome war and live together peacefully."

"Our history is long, but there is one event and one of our own kind that are of crucial importance in this respect," explained another of the Yorok crew. "Many thousands of years ago, our race was divided up much as yours is now. At that time, one of our people proposed a new teaching. This

Yorok said that if we want to have peace, we should do to others, what we want them to do to us. This seemed a most sensible suggestion, and since then we have worked hard at putting it into practice."

The silence that followed was long. The humans present glanced at one another, and although many of their jobs involved regular public speaking, none of them could find anything to say.

SOMEBODY UP THERE LIKES US

"So what is it that makes this case so unusual, doctor?" asked the captain of the Zog ship.

"Well, you know this single-celled organism that we discovered? It appears to be 'unwell', and yet the exact cause of the 'ailment' seems almost impossible to determine," replied the Zog expedition's chief scientist.

"Please, do explain further," said the ship's captain, genuinely interested in the life-form that they had discovered.

"As far as we can determine," the scientist explained, "this life form contains many different molecules that interact in a unique way, sometimes according to patterns, at other times seemingly quite chaotically. We believe we have identified the molecule that controls the transfer of cell resources to those molecules which in turn are responsible for producing the energy that is distributed throughout the cell, enabling the organism as a whole to continue to live, grow, and function. Yet while we were observing this and getting ready to write up a report, something peculiar happened. This key molecule suddenly stopped increasing its distribution of resources to the energy-production molecules in proportion to their needs. Within a few cycles, the other molecules in turn ceased to produce energy for the rest of the cell. We have no explanation for what has happened."

"Are you sure that in the process of your study you did not damage the cell or some important molecule?" the captain asked.

"Of course not!" retorted the chief scientist indignantly. "We took all the standard precautions. We have only observed, and have not interfered with the life form in any way. We simply cannot account for the behavior of the key resource-managing molecule, nor for that of the energy-producing molecules. The former is endangering the life of the whole, almost as though it had a will and were being stubborn. And the latter should still have had enough resources to continue producing energy for the cell, yet all their energy-producing activity has stopped entirely."

"Perhaps they are on strike," quipped the captain.

"Hmm! Must you be so crudely zogomorphic?" the scientist replied, becoming even more indignant. "This is a serious matter. This situation has already been going on for forty cycles, so the very existence of the life form may soon be at stake."

"Well, if it is a matter of life or death, then you must intervene," the captain said. "Do you have any suggestions, any intervention that you may be able to propose to remedy the situation?"

"There is one thing," said the scientist. "We observed in other parts of the cell, and in other molecular functions, a remarkable characteristic of this organism. When a molecule is removed or deteriorates, another molecule is found or produced to replace it. This suggests that, were we to remove the key resource-distribution molecule that appears to be the cause of the problem, it will be replaced with a healthy, effective one, and then everything should return to normal."

"Please doctor, do try it. It is our ethical duty," said the captain.

"OK, I'll send in a nano-probe with nano-tweezers, which should be able to accomplish this very quickly."

Slightly later, on Earth . . .

NEWS FLASH

The workers' strike that has been continuing non-stop for the past forty days at the World Energy Production Center ended abruptly today when the Center's director, who had refused to give in to workers' demands for an increase in salary, suddenly vanished from his office.

The director's secretary, who was the only eye-witness, is being subjected to psychiatric evaluation, having already been questioned by police. His remarkable account of events is that the director, Mr. Evan Jones, was pacing around his office when what looked like giant tweezers came through the window, grabbed Mr. Jones and carried him off out of sight. The possibility of foul play has not been ruled out, although security on site have confirmed that no unauthorized individuals were on the premises.

Meanwhile, the head of the Energy Workers' Union, Ms. Susan Simms, had this to say: "We consider this a satisfactory, if somewhat surprising, resolution to the crisis." When asked if she had any explanation to offer regarding this strange account of Mr. Jones' disappearance, she replied: "I guess somebody up there likes us."

BIBLIOGRAPHY

Alsford, Mike. *What If?: Religious Themes in Science Fiction*. London: Darton, Longman, and Todd, 2000.

Barad, Judith, and Ed Robertson. *The Ethics of Star Trek*. New York: HarperCollins, 2000.

Barbour, Ian. *When Science Meets Religion*. San Francisco: Harper Collins, 2000.

Bertonneau, Thomas, and Kim Paffenroth. *The Truth Is Out There: Christian Faith and the Classics of TV Science Fiction*. Grand Rapids: Brazos, 2006.

Bortolin, Matthew. *The Dharma of Star Wars*. Boston: Wisdom, 2005.

Bradbury, Ray. *The Illustrated Man*. Garden City: Doubleday, 1951.

Card, Orson Scott. *Maps in a Mirror*. New York: TOR, 1990.

Campbell, Joseph, and Bill Moyers. *The Power of Myth*. New York: Anchor, 1991.

Carroll, Noël, and Lester H. Hunt, eds. *Philosophy in the Twilight Zone*. Malden: Wiley-Blackwell, 2009.

Clarke, Arthur C. *Childhood's End*. New York: Ballantine, 1953.

Cowan, Douglas E. *Sacred Space: The Quest for Transcendence in Science Fiction Film and Television*. Waco: Baylor University Press, 2010.

Crome, Andrew, and James F. McGrath, eds. *Time and Relative Dimensions in Faith: Religion and Doctor Who*. London: Darton, Longman, and Todd, 2013.

Dann, Jack, ed. *Wandering Stars: An Anthology of Jewish Fantasy and Science Fiction*. Woodstock, VT: Jewish Lights, 1974.

Decker, Kevin S., and Jason T. Eberl, eds. *Star Wars and Philosophy*. Chicago: Open Court, 2005.

Bibliography

Dick, S. J., ed. *Many Worlds: The New Universe, Extraterrestrial Life, and the Theological Implications.* Philadelphia: Templeton Foundation, 2000.

Donaldson, Amy M. *We Want to Believe: Faith and Gospel in The X-files.* Eugene, OR: Cascade, 2011.

Eberl, Jason T., ed. *Battlestar Galactica and Philosophy.* Malden: Blackwell, 2008.

Ford, James E. "Battlestar Galactica and Mormon Theology." *Journal of Popular Culture* 17 (1983) 83–87.

Freud, Sigmund. *Civilization and its Discontents.* New York: Norton, 1961.

Garrett, Greg. *Holy Superheroes!* Colorado Springs: Pinon, 2005.

Geraci, Robert. "Robots and the Sacred in Science and Science Fiction: Theological Implications of Artificial Intelligence." *Zygon* 42.4 (December 2007) 961–80.

Gerrold, David, and Robert J. Sawyer, eds. *Boarding the Enterprise.* Dallas: BenBella, 2006.

Gould, Stephen Jay. "Nonoverlapping Magisteria." *Natural History* 106 (March 1997) 16–22.

Greenley, Andrew M., and Michael Cassutt, eds. *Sacred Visions.* New York: TOR, 1991.

Gregory, Alan P. R. *Science Fiction Theology: Beauty and the Transformation of the Sublime.* Waco: Baylor University Press, 2015.

Hanley, Richard. *The Metaphysics of Star Trek.* New York: Basic, 1997.

Hatch, Richard, ed. *So Say We All: An Unauthorized Collection of Thoughts and Opinions on Battlestar Galactica.* Dallas: BenBella, 2006.

Herbert, Frank. *Dune.* Philadelphia: Chilton, 1965.

Herzfeld, Noreen L. *In Our Image: Artificial Intelligence and the Human Spirit.* Minneapolis: Fortress, 2002.

Henderson, Mary. *Star Wars: The Magic of Myth.* New York: Bantam, 1997.

Hirt, Edward, and Joshua Clarkson. "The Psychology of Fandom: Understanding the Etiology, Motives, and Implications of Fanship." In *Consumer Behavior Knowledge for Effective Sports Marketing,* edited by Lynn R. Kahle and Angeline G. Close, 59–85. New York: Routledge, 2010.

Hrotic, Steven. *Religion in Science Fiction: The Evolution of an Idea and the Extinction of a Genre.* New York: Bloomsbury, 2014.

Irwin, William, ed. *The Matrix and Philosophy.* Chicago: Open Court, 2002.

————. *More Matrix and Philosophy: Revolutions and Reloaded Decoded*. Chicago: Open Court, 2005.

Jones, Timothy Paul. *Finding God in a Galaxy Far, Far Away*. Sisters: Multnomah, 2005.

Kaveney, Roz, and Jennifer Stoy, eds. *Battlestar Galactica: Investigating Flesh, Spirit, and Steel*. London: I. B. Tauris, 2010.

Kozlovic, Anton. "From Holy Aliens to Cyborg Saviours: Biblical Subtexts in Four Science Fiction Films." *Journal of Religion and Film* 5.2 (2001). Online: http://www.unomaha.edu/jrf/cyborg.htm.

Kraemer, Ross, William Cassidy, and Susan Schwartz. *Religions of Star Trek*. Boulder: Westview, 2001.

Kreuziger, Frederick A. *The Religion of Science Fiction*. Bowling Green, OH: Popular, 1986.

Kripal, Jeffrey. *Mutants and Mystics: Science Fiction, Superhero Comics, and the Paranormal*. Chicago: University of Chicago Press, 2011.

Layton, David. *The Humanism of Doctor Who: A Critical Study in Science Fiction and Philosophy*. Jefferson: McFarland, 2012.

Leonhardt, Jutta. *Jewish Worship in Philo of Alexandria*. TSAJ 84. Tübingen: Mohr-Siebeck, 2001.

Levinson, Paul, and Michael Waltemathe, eds. *Touching the Face of the Cosmos: On the Intersection of Space Travel and Religion*. New York: Fordham University Press, 2016.

Lewis, C. S. *Out of the Silent Planet*. New York: Macmillan, 1965.

Martin, Joel W., and Conrad E. Ostwalt, Jr. *Screening the Sacred: Religion, Myth, and Ideology in Popular American Film*. Boulder: Westview, 1995.

Mayo, Clark. *Kurt Vonnegut. The Gospels from Outer Space*. San Bernardino: Borgo, 1977.

McAvan, Emily. *The Postmodern Sacred: Popular Culture Spirituality in the Science Fiction, Fantasy and Urban Fantasy Genres*. Jefferson: McFarland, 2012.

McDowell, John C. *The Gospel According to Star Wars*. Louisville: Westminster John Knox, 2007.

McGrath, James F. "Monotheism." In *Vocabulary for the Study of Religion, Volume 2*, edited by Robert A. Segal and Kocku von Stuckrad, 470–74. Leiden: E. J. Brill, 2015.

————. "Religion and Science Fiction." In *Sense of Wonder: A Century of Science Fiction*, edited by Leigh Ronald Grossman, 394–96. Wildside, 2011.

————. "Religion, But Not As We Know It: Spirituality and Sci-Fi." In *Religion as Entertainment* edited by C. K. Robertson, 153–72. New York: Peter Lang, 2002.

————, ed. *Religion and Science Fiction*. Eugene, OR: Pickwick, 2011.

McKee, Gabriel. *The Gospel According to Science Fiction*. Louisville: Westminster John Knox, 2007.

————. *Pink Beams of Light from the God in the Gutter: The Science-fictional Religion of Philip K. Dick*. Lanham, MD: University Press of America, 2004.

Mohs, Mayo, ed. *Other Worlds, Other Gods*. New York: Avon, 1971.

Mountcastle, William W. *Science Fantasy Voices and Visions of Cosmic Religion*. Lanham, MD: University Press of America, 1996.

Murphy, George L. *Pulpit Science Fiction*. Lima: CSS, 2005.

Murphy, Nancy. "Jesus and Life on Mars." *The Christian Century* 113.31 (1996) 1028–29.

Nahin, Paul J. *Holy Sci-Fi! Where Science Fiction and Religion Intersect*. New York: Springer, 2014.

Piper, H. Beam. *Lord Kalvan of Otherwhen*. New York: Ace, 1965.

————. *Space Viking*. New York: Ace, 1963.

Porter, Jennifer, and Darcee McLaren, eds. *Star Trek and Sacred Ground: Explorations of* Star Trek, *Religion, and American Culture*. Albany: SUNY, 1999.

Reilly, Robert. *The Transcendent Adventure: Studies of Religion in Science Fiction/Fantasy*. Westport: Greenwood, 1985.

Rollins, James. *The Eye of God. A Sigma Force Novel*. New York: Harper Collins, 2013.

Russell, Mary Doria. *The Sparrow*. New York: Ballantine, 1996.

Sagan, Carl. *Contact*. New York: Simon and Schuster, 1986.

Sawyer, Robert J. *Calculating God*. New York: TOR, 2000.

Schneider, Susan, ed. *Science Fiction and Philosophy: From Time Travel to Superintelligence*. Malden: Wiley Blackwell, 2009.

Seay, Christopher and Greg Garrett. *The Gospel Reloaded: Exploring Spirituality and Faith in the Matrix*. Colorado Springs: Piñon, 2003.

Simmons, Dan. *Hyperion*. New York: Doubleday, 1989.

Steiff, Josef, and Tristan D. Tamplin, eds. *Battlestar Galactica and Philosophy: Mission Accomplished Or Mission Frakked Up?* Chicago: Open Court, 2008.

Tillich, Paul. *Dynamics of Faith*. New York: Harper & Row, 1957.

Warrick, Patricia, and Martin Harry Greenberg, eds. *The New Awareness: Religion Through Science Fiction*. New York: Delacorte, 1975.

Weber, David. *Honor of the Queen.* New York: Simon & Schuster, 1993.

Wetmore, Kevin J. *The Theology of Battlestar Galactica: American Christianity in the 2004–2009 Television Series.* Jefferson: McFarland, 2012.

Whitehead, Harriet. "Reasonably Fantastic: Some Perspectives on Scientology, Science Fiction, and Occultism." In *Religious Movements in Contemporary America,* edited by Irving I. Zaretsky and Mark P. Leone, 547–87. Princeton: Princeton University Press, 1974.

Wilkinson, David. *Alone in the Universe? The X-Files, Aliens and God.* Crowborough: Monarch, 1997.

———. *Power of the Force.* Lion, 2000.

———. "Star Wars: A Battle between the Cinema and the Church?" *The Plain Truth* (April-May 2000) 6–9.

Wimmler, Jutta. *Religious Science Fiction in Battlestar Galactica and Caprica: Women as Mediators of the Sacred and Profane.* Jefferson: McFarland, 2015.

Woodman, Tom. "Science Fiction, Religion and Transcendence." In *Science Fiction: A Critical Guide,* edited by Patrick Parrinder, 110–30. London: Longman, 1979.

Yeffeth, Glenn, ed. *Taking the Red Pill: Science, Philosophy and Religion in* The Matrix. Dallas: BenBella, 2003.

Zebrowski, George. *Macrolife.* New York: Harper & Row, 1979.

Made in the USA
Monee, IL
27 December 2023

50593537R00073